Belinda Copitch is a Third Culture Kid, having lived in three countries and eight cities. She has had innumerable careers – dental hygienist, charity director, and senior school teacher, amongst several. She currently works as a science teacher and a social science researcher, and her degrees include a B.Sc. in Microbiology, an M.Sc. in Molecular Parasitology and a PhD in Education. She lives in London.

This book is dedicated to my children, Justin and Kim, who put up with me gaining my education when I should have been a mother to them while they were gaining theirs. Despite me, they have both done admirably well, for which I am immensely proud. I love you guys, the families you have created and the choices you have made.

Belinda Copitch

COLLABORATION VERSUS COMPETITION

The Art of Working Together

AUSTIN MACAULEY PUBLISHERS™

LONDON • CAMBRIDGE • NEW YORK • SHARJAH

A CIP catalogue record for this title is available from the British Library.

ISBN 9781398462533 (Paperback)
ISBN 9781398462540 (ePub e-book)

www.austinmacauley.com

First Published 2023
Austin Macauley Publishers Ltd®
1 Canada Square
Canary Wharf
London
E14 5AA

Thank you to all my former line managers and employers for helping me to recognise what it means to be a good leader – some more unwittingly than by design. Thank you to all my former colleagues and reportees who enabled me to understand leadership and grow as a professional. To all those who appear as fictionalised versions of yourselves and your companies, I am grateful to have been your colleague or that you agreed to let me to interview you. I have learned from each and every one of you.

Special thanks to Sharyn Seidel who designed the fabulous cover for me. It feels very special for me to have my dear school friend from fifty years ago be a part of this project. Her abiding friendship after several decades is truly valued.

Glenda Sacks Jaffe deserves a special note of thanks for really detailed editing, critiquing and proofreading in record time. She and I crossed the borders of time and space together having been childhood friends in Cape Town fifty years ago, and she now lives in San Diego. Her comments from across the Atlantic were inordinately helpful.

Joanna Brown's proofreading is much appreciated. She gave me some useful pointers in the process.

I am very grateful to Beverley Shrand who introduced me to Systems Thinking at a Limmud conference several years ago. I subsequently asked her for her notes and never realised until years later that I was going to use what I learned from her in my book.

Table of Contents

1. Why Is Competition the Accepted Norm?

Definition: Competition arises when two or more parties strive for a goal or reward which cannot be shared.

This results in one winner and the remainder being disappointed.

"Competition has been shown to be useful up to a certain point and no further, but cooperation, which is the thing we must strive for today, begins where competition leaves off."

Franklin D Roosevelt

We have grown up thinking and believing that competition is motivational, and helps us to succeed. We want to do better than Johnny in that English test; we want to attract that person of the opposite sex who only has eyes for the exceptional beauty; if you ever surfed, you lost out on the good waves to those who muscled in first; if the bus or train you were waiting for was full to capacity, you lost a place to those who forced their way on when it came to your station.

However, life isn't a collection of anecdotes. Let's look at it this way.

Remember the days when you were in primary school and had to take part in the school sports day. Harry ALWAYS won the running race and there seemed no point in even entering. Nonetheless, you were told by your class teacher that you were good enough to enter. She was showing faith in your abilities and encouraging you to participate. In reality, there wasn't a race if everybody chose not to compete against Harry. You entered because of her encouragement, because they needed to populate the field.

You entered; you ran; you came in somewhere in the middle of the pack. No rosettes, no mentions, no congratulations – despite the fact that you gave it your all and are really proud of the fact that you ran your best ever, and you had successfully overtaken some of the pack to improve your usual record of coming in in the last quartile. The lack of recognition of your personal achievement left you feeling unmotivated, despondent and impotent. In this way you were trained to believe that you had to beat Harry to be a success, to attain recognition and rewards. In essence, the only way you were going to receive the recognition for your achievement was to come in the first three places.

It was the same when they were handing out accolades for good academic achievements. If you weren't performing amongst the best in the class, you were lost in the milieu, your personal battles and achievements ignored and trampled on in the rush to congratulate Bertha and Simon for attaining 80% or above. No-one recognised that your achievement of 56% represented a hard slog and a personal best. No one patted you on the back and commended you for your effort. No one motivated you to do better, by recognising your achievement.

I once sat in an organisational team meeting for all of the 50 staff in a charity I was working for. We had just appointed a new CEO whose manner and approach had led us to believe that we were heading away from our hitherto departmental approach towards collaboration based on good interdepartmental cooperation and building of relationships.

I was excited to be attending our first full staff meeting where I was looking forward to her espousing her new policy of teamwork, empathetic environment and reciprocal learning.

I have never been so demoralised in all of my working life as when she proceeded to describe a new policy she was implementing. She would be rewarding good work with a cheap promotional pen. Here was the CEO of a large national NFP handing out primary school rewards to her colleagues for doing their jobs. She then proceeded to present the first such pen to one of my colleagues for fulfilling his work as the finance director, producing the accounts on time – as he had every year since he had been there. She was rewarding him for doing his job. FOR DOING HIS JOB!

Not only was he being paid for doing the accounts, and doing what we expect him to do, but what irked me the most was that there were forty-nine people sitting in that circle that afternoon, all needing to have their work recognised, all doing their job, and many of them doing it exceptionally well. Most of them were the admin and ancillary staff, the support personnel. Not members of the directorial team, as was the gentleman who won the first such accolade.

And, anyway who has meetings with 50 people in a circle? This was her way of demonstrating that no-one should be in front, no-one excluded or made to feel secondary. We had to borrow a very large hall for this meeting.

I had worked in the organisation for several years and, as regional director, I had always made a point of working collaboratively and cross-departmentally – both in the regions and with my London colleagues. I knew the calibre of every single person in that room and I knew that there were people there on much lower salaries who were doing sterling work, achieving phenomenal results and always delivering on time and in budget; many going above and beyond because they believed in the organisation. The likelihood of any of them ever getting the acknowledgement from the new CEO seemed slim to me as she handed her first pen to one of the most senior people in the organisation. I did a quick calculation. Even if she decided on a policy of making sure that everyone had a turn to receive a pen at the quarterly meetings, it would take twelve-and-a-half years before the last person received theirs. And how would you feel if you were waiting all those years for what you know you deserved – even after two years? Indeed, recognition that you deserved every single day.

The reason I relate this story is because I believe it illustrates how competition only serves to make everyone but the front runner feel bad about themselves. I believe that this strategy left the bulk of the staff feeling dejected, unrecognised and frustrated. Yes, it may make them strive harder for recognition but, in doing so, they are feeling pretty rotten about themselves, feeling that they are under-achieving, not attaining the results they are striving for and certainly not getting the recognition for the good work that they are doing. People have to jostle in line just to attain the recognition that their system should be providing on a daily basis.

We don't need a cheap reward; what we need is regular affirmation that we are doing a good job; we need assistance and advice when it is called for; we need novel ideas when we have exhausted all of those in our head; we need praise and motivation. Daily. Those are the forces which make our efforts both more successful and productive, and create a more pleasant work environment. We all need acknowledgement. Without it we are constantly questioning whether we have fulfilled the remit, whether we are good enough or whether our output is sufficient. We shouldn't have to stand in line for recognition. Each and every one of us in an organisation should be receiving it and issuing it often.

A 2015 Gallup poll found that 67% of employees whose managers communicated their strengths were fully engaged in their work, as compared to 31% of employees whose managers only communicated their weaknesses. (https://www.gallup.com/workplace/236570/employees-lotmanagers.aspx) Praise matters. Even acknowledgement matters.

Unsurprisingly, this CEO didn't see out the year in the organisation. She had phenomenal interpersonal skills, empathy and compassion, but she was severely lacking in leadership skills. By this I mean that she failed to see the worth in her staff and spectacularly failed to demonstrate that she appreciated their contribution.

I once saw an interview with Dr Ramani Durvasula (https://www.youtube.com/watch?v=_uJs0iGQN0M&t=25s) who is an expert on narcissism. She claims that agreeable people are less recognised and less well paid than their narcissistic (competitive, pushy, self-aggrandising) counterparts. The world of work is populated by narcissists, and this is the model that we as a society are used to seeing. She said, "If I wrote a book on the narcissist, it becomes the 'How To Guide for how to achieve' in the new world order." So, entrenched in our society is the notion that competitiveness is the best way to achieve results.

So, we are hoodwinked into thinking that we have to compete against each other, that our working environment is akin to that primary school running race, everyone striving for first place. In fact, we are failing to acknowledge that we are part of an entity (business, charity, organisation) which has to take first place. I like to visualise this as Atlas holding up the Earth. All of the staff come together to form a solitary Atlas, holding up the Earth. If any one of us doesn't strive for the best, it is the business that suffers and flounders, not any of the individuals. If Atlas only puts his effort into one hand, the Earth falls; if he doesn't strengthen his stance with both feet, the Earth falls. All members of the team play a part and all members of the team deserve full and constant recognition for the part that they play. They should not be competing against each other; they should be striving for the perfection of the organisation. More importantly, we should engender an environment where they want to do that.

Even though it is impressed upon us from a young age, I find from my professional experience in the classroom that collaboration is much more valued by the students than competition. If you set an individual creative task to a group of students, they will inevitably coalesce to form cooperative groups, borrowing ideas, sharing thoughts and offering assistance to each other. Usually, when I set them an individual task, there will be at least one pupil who raises the question of whether they are allowed to work together.

If you go into a branch of any fast-food establishment, you see the board with 'Employee of the week'. I despair. I am sure it is not confined to fast food businesses. It is an endemic practice. All I see in the subtext is all the employees whose hard work was not recognised, workers who strive constantly to be agreeable and amenable, employees who follow instructions and do the best that they can without any of that being recognised for what it is, rather than compared with the work of someone else. In fact, you may achieve 'employee of the week' status one week, perform to exactly the same standards the following week and not get recognised. It's someone else's turn.

I stress, we all need recognition, all the time.

2. Competition Is an Age-Old Way of Seeing the World

"Companies that focus solely on competition will ultimately die. Those that focus on value creation will thrive."

Edward de Bono

We all know that there are fundamentals for which we compete. Biologists have known for hundreds of years that organisms compete for food, a mate, shelter; in some cases, even air and space (such as bacterial populations).

This concept conjures up visions of the cave man going out and hunting a large prey and bringing it back to his family to consume. He has to find and kill the available prey before the next clan can get to it.

We can think about the visions we have of animals competing for a mate. For instance, peacocks with their elaborate display of feathers, lions with their impressive manes, chimps fighting for supremacy.

These examples give us the notion that the animal kingdom is inherently competitive and that we need to compete in everything we do, including the workplace.

In fact, this is never how it was. Even if we look at animals in the wild, examples of communal living and cooperation abound.

Take hyenas for instance. We might think of them as lone stalkers, pouncing on their prey independently. However, nothing could be further from the truth. Hyenas hunt in packs. When a prey is spotted, hyenas will communicate with each other by growling, barking and screeching. This attracts more hyenas. Each hyena knows what role he plays and where he should be stationed in relation to the prey. In this way they are able to capture prey which is significantly larger than an individual hyena. When there is a sufficiently co-ordinated mob, they have even been known to successfully attack a lion.

Chimps reward altruism and punish non-cooperation. When we do see violent behaviour amongst chimps, it is usually directed at a member of the community who is not pulling its weight. Research has time and again shown that chimps prefer to work cooperatively and display qualities of altruism which ultimately lead to mutual benefit. They usually make helpful choices more readily than selfish ones. They also teach other skills and pass them down the generations.

Examining a chimp population, we can see the breakdown of duties in a commune. The social order is very organised. The alpha male presides over his community ensuring that every member plays an appropriate role. Some are rearing young; some foraging and some hunting. There is conservation of heat when necessary, by keeping close together, and chimps groom each other to remove ectoparasites such as ticks and fleas. Females are given first access to food, to ensure that the young are well nourished.

These are all examples of how the colony lives and functions collaboratively for the success of the whole community.

There are even many examples of interspecies cooperation. For instance, ravens guide wolves to potential prey. Badgers and coyotes help each other out. Coyotes can outrun their small mammal prey, but when the prey burrows underground, the badger can dig them out. And, of course, let's look at our own domestic dog. In exchange for being a seeing-eye dog, or other working dog, or even just a companion, dogs gain shelter and food.

Humans have evolved to be communal. Work tasks and roles are shared across society, child-rearing is pooled (for example, nurseries, schools), food capture is commercial, healthcare is provided by specialists. In small rural villages we see collective food capture and preparation. Even in urban society, those who live in extended three-generation families are the most efficient and effective at organising their lives.

So why do we persist in our need for competition in the workplace? The truth is that winning undoubtedly feels good, and we are all trying to achieve that feel-good factor. However, it denigrates all those who didn't win. And there are far more of them in any team than the single winner. What we are doing is creating a disgruntled workforce.

Let's go back to the CEO who gave out a promotional pen. The recipient felt good, acknowledged and accomplished; forty-nine other people felt that their work was worthless, unrecognised and unappreciated.

I have witnessed many exercises that trainers or managers routinely use in team training events to augment team-player attitudes. For instance:

- Spaghetti tower: teams compete to build the tallest possible tower out of spaghetti and marshmallows (which encourages lateral thinking and co-operative attitudes).
- The great egg drop: teams compete to construct an effective form of packaging to prevent an egg from breaking when being dropped.
- Escape Rooms (a fun way to engender team work).

There are many others in the same vein. These activities engender a lot of fun and bond the individual teams. However, they do rely, for maximum enjoyment, on the element of competition. One team has to win, and let's remember that when someone wins, others have to lose. Individuals in the team will be valued relative to their respective contributions.

Tool

There are also many things that you can do with your team to improve their engagement and to engender a team spirit that don't involve competition, but do bond the team.

- Recommend a particular TED talk on a weekly basis, and exchange opinions and analysis about it
- Outings
- Adopt a charity – either for material or practical help
- Yoga/Mindfulness sessions
- Learn a language or new skill together
- Take it in turns for each member of the team to bring ten minutes of learning to every team meeting.

The list is endless.

There are many creative activities that are potentially far more collaborative or conducive to team building. Projects, such as clean-up of a local beauty spot is non-competitive and promotes teamwork, but also has the feel-good factor of achieving something for the community, and it is a very good promotional activity for the company. The project often goes on long after the initial activity.

I have even heard of companies that allot one day a week/fortnight/month to work on anything you want. The idea is that people are able to pursue their pet projects or passions, and if only one thing in ten works out for the company, it's still a gain, and one that could never have been achieved if everyone was working according to their structured remit and in their silos.

Exercise:

Each individual in the team is instructed to bring a piece of music to the session. One at a time each individual plays their piece of music, following which they describe why they brought that particular piece. They then field questions from the rest of the team. Depending on time constraints and numbers in the team, the music pieces can either be whole tracks or small sections. Questions can be a free-for-all or a managed forum. They can be limited to three questions per participant or as many as arise.

<u>Benefits:</u>

- The exercise generates team bonding through getting to know some intimate details of their colleagues – what excites them, what they enjoy, the genre of music they prefer, and their reasons for bringing that particular track. It gives a window to their persona outside of work.
- Participants benefit the rest of the team paying them attention and taking a genuine interest in what they are presenting.
- The exercise itself is pleasant. Who doesn't like listening to music?
- There is an added bonus of being introduced to new music, which is always a pleasant experience when it is music that you take to.
- Team members find out commonalities with colleagues when they follow or enjoy similar music.

People in the organisation whom you have never talked to before can become your friends by learning more about them.

- Team members are able to glean information from their colleagues when they have an opportunity to ask them questions about their choice. This can be really helpful in the workplace.
- The session ends with everybody knowing a little bit more about each other.

3. Times Change: Organisations Need to Change

"Progress is impossible without change; and those who cannot change their minds cannot change anything."

George Bernard Shaw

I used to work in a charity delivering community development. I would go into different communities, assess their needs and help them to understand how they can use their own resources to increase capacity, raise their profile and promote engagement.

I would first observe the community and interview the leaders and the members of a community at work, to begin to gain an understanding. I would often then continue my evaluation of the community by facilitating a focus group or some sort of exercise to elicit information and promote dialogue. Once having identified the key areas to address, I would set them a task to allow the community members to develop the conversation and explore the issues at hand in ways that they might not have considered.

On one such occasion, while the members of the community were assembled and beginning to engage with the task I had set them, I quietly slipped into the kitchen to help those who had volunteered to make the refreshments for the lunchtime break. There I found a handful of ladies (why is it always the ladies?) preparing sandwiches and fruit platters. I rolled up my proverbial sleeves and started to assist. No sooner had I started my first batch of sandwiches, and was beginning to cut them up to place on the serving trays, than I was confronted by one of the ladies, "We don't cut our sandwiches on the diagonal, we cut them across to make rectangles." I was shocked. Not only was this a pettiness that I was not expecting, but it perfectly illustrated to me the intractability of the community to change and to the notion of new ideas and innovation. The philosophy of "we've always done it this way" was pervasive in every aspect of community life. Change, however trivial, is traumatic.

Traditions are often dearly held in many organisations, without knowing the background or reason for their inception. "This is the way we do things" is a common refrain and one that is embedded in many an organisation. It is time to stop and ask why. Traditions, by definition, hold people and organisations back. They prevent change, or development of progress. They keep people blindly doing the same things – often even expecting to get different results.

Story:

In the '70s I used to belong to a youth organisation that held annual summer camps. The long-drop blocks were called the "plyms". Nobody knew why, but it was an esotericism (probably a euphemism) which we all employed. Every year we would arrive at the campsite and invoke our esoteric language for the toilet block. Generations of members knew the word and so it got passed down.

It wasn't until about thirty years later that I discovered the word's origin from someone who had been involved.

In the early '60s the organisation had just bought the campsite and was putting everything into place for the first cohort of campers to attend. They needed something to provide privacy for the toilet block. Someone hit on a bright idea. They would head down to the docks and pick up a large crate of the sort that cars were shipped in. They arrived back on the site with a large crate and proceeded to saw off the top, upending it and carving a door, to create housing for the long drop. The carving had split through the name of the car that had been housed within – Plymouth, leaving just the word Plym, looking like a label on the side of the crate.

Just a cute illustration of how traditions and language are passed down beyond their period of relevance without anyone ever retaining the significance.

Some traditions can be good. They promote uniformity, identity and belonging. They help people to know what is expected of them, where they fit in in the scheme of the organisation, and what the measures of success are. Overall, though, traditions that are meaningless (such as the shape of our sandwiches) are going to stymie development.

The types of change we need to welcome are manifold. Technology, Attitudes and even Attire in the workplace today would be completely alien to someone time travelling from even ten years ago.

Technology

Technology has moved on incredibly since I started my first job. Mobile phones, social media, communication apps, preservation of data (amongst many others) have all completely changed the way that we work. Let's take my very first professional job as a part-time dental nurse while I was still at school.

I would phone each patient up the day before to remind them of their appointment. This would take me several hours. Today, I would send a mass mail-merge message to the mobile phones of every patient in a matter of minutes.

I would manually chart the status of every tooth according to the dentist's evaluation. Today, it would all be on a computer from the last time, and I could make simple adjustments from the extant document.

Patient notes would go missing or get misfiled, or pages would drop out. Today, it is all saved on a hard drive, backups made on a regular basis, and instantly retrievable.

X-rays would be taken onto silver backed photographic paper, accumulated through the day and then the whole day's x-rays would be developed together in the dark room, and then hung to dry. A process which would take several hours and result in the dentist not being able to discuss the treatment plan with the patient until at least the following day, when he had access to the developed x-rays. Today the x-ray is instantly viewable on the computer screen once taken.

Referring a patient to a specialist such as an endodontist would require a letter to be sent in the post with an enclosed x-ray, mounted on a card for preservation. This required two x-rays to be taken each time – one for the referral and one for the files. Today an e-mail can be instantly zapped to the specialist with the attached x-ray that was taken moments earlier.

I could go on, but you get the picture. Technology has changed how we work to the point that our jobs would be unrecognisable to previous generations. We need to embrace that, and accept that the rate of change has increased exponentially in some spheres. We need to respect that some colleagues may not have the up-to-date, state-of-the-art comfort with technology that others do.

A simple example of how technology can sometimes impede us is the way that we file things. For instance, minute taking. Before computers, we would diligently file our new set of minutes in the appropriate cabinet folder in date order. You would have a large filing cabinet with a folder called Board Meetings. Within that folder would be subfolders for each year. Then the monthly meetings would be filed in the appropriate year chronologically. Simple.

Today, I have found many offices which simply file on computer within a named folder. So, for instance, you might have a folder called 'Board Meetings', within which you might store the various sets of minutes, perhaps naming them 'minutes – 1st June 2020'. They are then stored alphanumerically, and may take a while to find, because they are not labelled explicitly enough. Sometimes, they are filed as 'Board meeting 1', 'Board meeting 2' etc. I have been in a situation where I had to open and read several such documents before I was able to find the one I was looking for.

> **Technique:** Younger members of the team might realise that by simply filing under the backwards date and description, all documents will be lined up in the correct chronological order and rendered easy to find– e.g. The minutes of a Board meeting on June 1st 2022 would be:
>   '220601 Board minutes'
>   Not only is chronological filing attained, but the label instantly indicates the exact date of the meeting.

Attire

Dressing for work has fundamentally changed. I often go into work environments where staff are wearing jeans. Many large organisations favour the 'dress down Friday' policy. They find that the ability to wear less formal clothes encourages a relaxed attitude and promotes a more pleasant work environment. People not only feel more relaxed in less formal clothing but they also get to express their identity. This in itself creates new alliances among the staff.

I have been into schools where the support staff (and sometimes the teaching staff, too) are in very casual clothes such as jeans. What I have observed is that the members of staff in casual clothes tend to have an affinity with the pupils. Youngsters see them as closer to them than the teaching staff, and are more inclined to listen to them as an ally rather than as a teacher who they often see as an adversary.

I once worked in a company where the CEO was very prescriptive about the dress code. Staff were admonished if they didn't wear a suit or jacket. He ran a very tight ship, with the result that employees were disgruntled and felt controlled and straightjacketed. Looser attitudes to dress results in a more relaxed and creative atmosphere.

Take the big social media companies, for instance. There is no dress code whatsoever and there is a very relaxed attitude to parameters and boundaries. Employees are encouraged to collaborate across departments and to make associations which might not come naturally in a more formal environment. This self-expression results in staff feeling more comfortable in promoting their ideas however 'out there' they may be.

You may have noticed that doctors have stopped wearing ties. This was originally a cross-infection prevention measure. The tie is handled multiple times when tying it; it dangles over the patient when she is being examined; it may brush against multiple sources of infection or contamination during the course of the day. However, by not wearing a tie, the doctors have placed themselves on a more informal footing with their patients. People feel more comfortable in airing their concerns to someone who is 'like them', not formal, patronising or superior.

Attitudes

There was a time when one respected one's elders regardless. We deferred to their experience and gave credence to their perceived wisdom. Whilst this did keep an organised social order, it often led to frustrations and lack of vision.

Youngsters with new ideas were ignored in favour of older colleagues. Thankfully, in our more enlightened times, we recognise that novel solutions can often be found by using the fresh outlook of the newcomer.

Work ethic has changed dramatically, too. Youngsters begin their professional careers by having an expectation of time off for holidays and medical appointments. Some people are first out of the door when it comes to home time. Much of the work day is spent on checking in on social media, personal messages and phone calls. Whilst work-life balance may be important, there seems to be little in this attitude which translates to dedication to the employer. When we take time off, or when we slack in what we offer during the day, it is not just the business or organisation that suffers. What happens is that our colleagues have to step in and do some of the extra work which we have not completed.

Some of the new big social media companies are changing this. LinkedIn, for instance doesn't monitor holidays or work hours, as long as the work gets done. They appreciate that their workers work best at their own pace and by setting their own parameters. In so doing, they have created a dedicated workforce who enjoy being in their employ. Just a quick glance at LinkedIn's website will reveal a page with a vast array of perks and benefits of working for the company. On their website, is this quotation from an employee:

"I'm excited to come into work every day because of the talented, passionate people I'm surrounded by, all of whom are striving towards a shared vision of creating economic opportunity for the global workforce. Day-to-day challenges tend to look pretty trivial when we're focused on helping change the world."

(careers.linkedin.com/)

This is the attitude that we all want to engender in the workplace.

Gone are the days when playing the despot in the workplace gets results. All it does is alienate the workforce and create disgruntled and unmotivated employees.

Today's managers are successful when they facilitate, encourage and engage their employees. Respect is no longer deserved through status, but earned by offering respect first.

In order to explore the root causes of a problem in the workplace, an ideal technique is to use Systems Thinking, a collaborative means of exploring and incorporating the entire team's individual ideas and perspectives.

Tool: Systems Thinking

Systems thinking enables a team to explore the root causes of complex problems, enabling all voices to be heard, valued and evaluated. It enables a team to prioritise, by understanding the forces which are causing issues, or around which other issues are focused.

The beauty of a systems thinking approach is that it is a great way to stimulate dialogue and prompt exchange of ideas and opinions. It allows individuals to voice their opinions and to have those opinions respectfully deliberated.

Additionally, it enables the team to appreciate multiple perspectives and to engage with each on multiple levels, to arrive at a collaborative outlook.

When using a systems thinking approach hidden assumptions can be exposed and evaluated effectively. By doing so, group learning is enhanced leading to a shared understanding of an issue. This engenders team loyalty and shared ownership of a plan.

Definition: A system is any entity that is made up of parts that interact.

Systems thinking is a wonderful tool for elucidating the root causes of a complex problem. It employs 'Zooming out' or looking at how other aspects outside of a project's traditional boundaries will impact on or influence the success of the project. Zooming out helps one to see the interactions between factors and to identify the causal relationships.

The first task is to identify the parts of a system, before finding out how they interrelate.

By examining each relationship in turn, it is possible to very quickly gain an in-depth understanding of the necessary interventions, policies and patterns, in order to develop the values and perspectives. This helps to gain perspective of each of the factors individually as well as of the system as a whole.

The stages in the process are:

1. Define the problem
2. Identify the factors
3. Elucidate the relationships
4. Identify the drivers and outcomes

Here's how it works:

Start with a title on a large flipchart. For our example, we will use the following rubric: How can we expand the use of the web to increase sales leads?

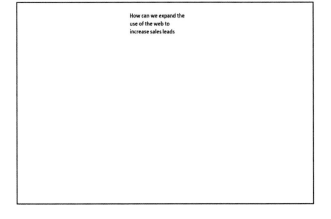

Divide your team into pairs and ask the pairs to come up with all of the elements of the system that might play an influential role. Each pair writes each element on a separate Post-it note. Once this has been done, the team comes back together and agrees on the elements that are important. There may be duplicates or similar concepts which need to be consolidated. There may be some that are not relevant.

Place the Post-It notes on the flip chart in a circle in any order.

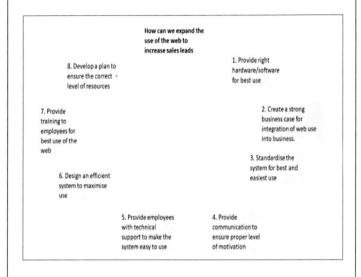

Now you will produce an interrelationship digraph.

Consider the relationship between the first Post-it note and all of the others in turn, one pair at a time.

Use an 'influence' arrow to connect factors. The arrows should be drawn from the factor that influences to the one being influenced.

If both influence each other, draw that arrow to reflect the stronger influence. No two factors should have arrows in both directions

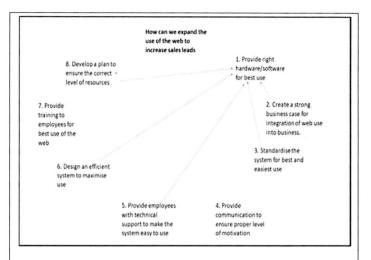

Work systematically – e.g. working round the circle in a clockwise direction until all of the elements have an arrow between all the others.

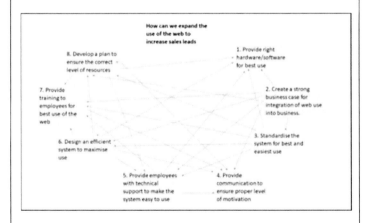

Once all the factors have a relationship arrow drawn between them and each of the others, count the number of in and out arrow for each factor.

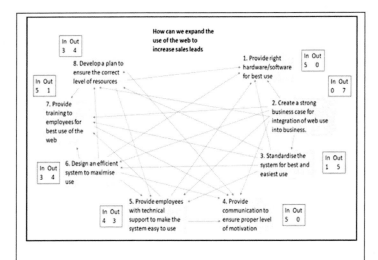

How can we expand the use of the web to increase sales leads

In Out
3   4

8. Develop a plan to ensure the correct level of resources

In Out
5   1

7. Provide training to employees for best use of the web

In Out
3   4

6. Design an efficient system to maximise use

In Out
4   3

5. Provide employees with technical support to make the system easy to use

4. Provide communication to ensure proper level of motivation

In Out
5   0

3. Standardise the system for best and easiest use

In Out
1   5

2. Create a strong business case for integration of web use into business.

In Out
0   7

1. Provide right hardware/software for best use

In Out
5   0

The factors with more outgoing arrows will be 'root causes' or 'drivers'. Those with more incoming arrows are called 'outcomes'

We now have a list of drivers which we can prioritise

Drivers	Outcomes
• Create a strong business case for integration of web use into business. • Standardise the system for best and easiest use. • Design an efficient system to maximise use. • Develop a plan to ensure the	• Provide right hardware/ software for best use • Provide communication to ensure proper level of communication • Provide employees with technical support to make the system easy to use • Provide training for employees for best use of the web

| correct level of resources | • Develop a plan to ensure the correct level of resources. |

Systems thinking is an excellent way to incorporate collaborative techniques to generate an understanding of what the root causes of a problem are and develop a strategy for addressing them. It unifies a team in creating a plan of action which the entire team has had a hand in creating.

4. Creating a Team Culture

"Great things in business are never done by one person, they're done by a team of people."

Steve Jobs

Team culture is vital for any company. It promotes cohesion, bonds the staff through a shared ethos, and provides the grounding on which staff know how to behave.

Definition: Team culture is the collection of shared attitudes, behaviours and beliefs to which a group of individuals adhere. At best it unifies a group of people.

Bonding

We need a team culture because it sets the boundaries and goals for individuals to work within and to know the norms of conduct and performance. Having an overt team culture is essential for bonding amongst the team members and bonding, in turn, is essential for loyalty, consistency and dependency. It helps a team to work well together, engenders a happy workplace environment, and increases productivity. It is also essential as a division of labour. All team members bring different skills and experience to the team. Creating a cohesive team means effective distribution of roles.

When I was in my first professional job as a teenager, I worked as a dental nurse. The first practice I worked in had a standard hierarchical structure where everyone knew their place and the practice principal made all the decisions. Any job that I have subsequently worked in with this model had the same consequences, namely a 'we-they' situation. The staff badmouthed the leadership and vice versa. There was an adversarial attitude between management and staff. This is not a healthy work environment; it doesn't promote loyalty, and the result is a quick staff turnover. This is not only unpleasant but is expensive, disruptive and stultifying for business development.

Team Building

There are many team building exercises that bring teams together.

In another job, I worked for a team where we were regularly treated to evenings out by the leadership. These outings were occasions such as theatre evenings or restaurant meals. Through these off-site events, we created real relationships across the teams and across the hierarchy, we knew the people behind the role, and we had each other's backs when we returned to the workplace. This was no longer just a professional attitude, but a genuine concern for each other's welfare and workload. It resulted in a confidence to propose suggestions or ideas without the fear of being ignored or dismissed. This, too was a dental practice. However, unlike the former, we had regular innovations, constant upgrading of work conditions and a sense of mutual ownership of the ethos and culture. This translated to happy staff and leaders, content patients and an all-round sense of accomplishment and achievement. It was a great place to work.

Some might say that investing time in team building is unproductive, expensive and time-wasting, time that could otherwise be spent on the job in hand – on sourcing new clients, on improving work environment, on delivering to the clients or stakeholders. However, in creating a team whose members have each other's best interests at heart, we are creating a team whose members help each other out. Individuals are less likely to 'pull a sicky' because they know that it is their colleagues who will have to take up the slack or cover the work that they are not doing. Far from reducing productivity, a day or evening out can boost productivity, enhance loyalty and reduce staff erosion. Managers and staff are no longer adversarial, but part of a greater whole, no longer having a sense of knowing their place (implying a static position), but now understanding the part that their colleagues play in oiling the organisational cogs (implying that the inter-relationships are fluid, and that every member of staff has agency).

Engendering Loyalty

Agency is important. People who feel that they are lacking control will be frustrated and unmotivated. Persistent lack of control of our lives can lead to depression, anxiety, anger and a whole host of other mental health issues or emotional concerns and unease. People who are in control are happy people, and happy people are a positive force in any organisation.

I know a young woman in her mid-twenties who left her previous job where she was very successful and highly regarded both by her managers and her peers. She left due to just such concerns of lack of control. Nobody likes to be a puppet, even when you are really good at it. She is now in a new organisation, in a relatively junior role. However, her new boss is constantly challenging her, always putting her just out of her comfort zone so that she picks up new skills or tools to do the job better. This is confidence boosting and empowering. Her line manager is creating a new source of leadership. Instead of knocking her for what she has done wrong, or finding holes in her output as so many managers do, her new manager is creating a highly skilled workforce with loyalty and reliability.

I once held a training day for a large charity who were all there in pairs comprised of a voluntary leader and someone working within the branch, from different regional branches. The introduction to my first session was a simple exercise.

Introductory exercise:

1. Individuals write down 5 good characteristics/behaviours that they have noticed about their colleague/team partner that make them a good leader.
2. They exchange these thoughts with each other and identify what makes the pair work well as a team.
3. In plenary – summarise that we all have different skills which we dovetail to make a good leadership team.

I was running this day with a colleague and zapped her the first draft of my session plans a week or so before the event. She e-mailed me straight back with two questions about my intro:

1. Didn't you mean to write 'bad' rather than 'good'?
2. Didn't you mean to write 'co-worker' rather than 'leader'?

No, I meant both. Firstly, by accentuating what our co-workers are good at, we show them that we value their input, we trust them to do their job well and we have confidence in them. This not only bolsters their confidence but ensures their loyalty to the person who believes in them.

But why did I use the word 'leader'? After all it might have been an administrator, a volunteer or any other functionary who was being addressed. By asserting (albeit covertly) that they are all leaders, I have bolstered their confidence, empowered them to take action and set them on the leadership trajectory (even if they were not on that pathway already). By identifying as leaders, they **become** leaders.

Skill Sharing

When teams come together, or individuals work together across teams, magic happens. New ideas surface, novel solutions are born, and staff members move further and learn more than they possibly could on their own.

The great Russian social scientist, Lev Vygotsky developed his theory of the 'Zone of Proximal Development' (ZPD) to explain how this works.

Definition: The Zone of Proximal Development refers to the gap between extant knowledge or abilities and what can be learned or achieved with the help of someone else.

In its most basic situation, we see how a child learns. Learning almost always occurs in the presence, or under the tutelage of an adult. The child needs instruction from someone more knowledgeable than themselves in order to develop and learn.

However, the ZPD can also be invoked in many other situations, other than traditional learning. The traditional model of the workplace was that you put all the people who worked in the same field, had the same skills or shared the same knowledge into the same team. Here they all agreed with each other, nodded sagely at their teammates' ideas and production, bonded over shared world views and churned out the same mind-numbing work and ideas over and over again.

What if we mix our teams up? We put the IT boffin with the HR manager, with the educator ... and soon you have a team who can share their knowledge with each other, develop new ideas based on the collective wisdom, and innovate based on the combined knowledge and expertise. This is harnessing the ZPD to its best effect. Each member of this team is learning from the others. Each person is pushing their Zone of Proximal Development further out to acquire new knowledge and skills. Each individual is excited to be incorporating new ideas, systems or methods into their repertoire.

Mixing your team to harness the ZPD is like adding colour to a table. Tables are usually two dimensional; two axes convey two axioms of information. By adding colour, you immediately enable a third dimension to be presented. Skill sharing adds colour to your team's environment.

Example: A table with three dimensions.

Wikipedia has a simple table with which it exemplifies the term, 'table'. Columns labelled 'First name', 'Last name' and 'Age'. We could keep adding columns. For example, gender, location etc. What if we wanted to add weight groups, for instance? We want to see at a glance which individuals are in the same category. We could add another column, but we could add a new dimension. We could have each weight range represented by a different colour. We can then immediately pick out all the reds, yellows or greens to assign weight appropriate health regimes or diets.

Group Dynamics

Derek Pugh wrote widely about group dynamics. He was an organisational psychologist and professor of Organisational Development. I read a paper of his way back in the 70s where he espoused the theory that every group is made up of 'characters'. You know the ones; there's the 'clown' who quips about everything, the 'confessor' who dominates the floor with personal examples; the 'gate-keeper' who assimilates all of the information shared into a cogent thesis … and so on. This was received wisdom back then. Every team or group that we entered would offer the same characters, each fulfilling a role in assembling the group.

We've probably all experienced it and can name the person in each group that we are a part of who fulfils each role.

But here's the thing. My own research suggests that we are not stuck in a rigid role of character and behaviour. We adapt. For every group and situation we are in, we display a different facet of ourselves, depending on the needs of the group and the other characters. So, I might be the clown in one group but the negativist in another and the interrupter in a third. I see it as a giant polyhedron, with each of my potential characteristics written on a facet. As I enter a situation, my polyhedron swivels and turns until settling on my appropriate facet for the group I am in.

This adaptation is important to keep in mind. If we go into a setting with a preconceived idea of how everyone is going to behave, we are just rubber-stamping the outcomes of the meeting. Why not utilise the polyhedron? Encourage different facets to be displayed. Encourage your team members by asking questions that force them to adopt a different facet. Invite them to offer solutions that are only positive, for instance.

Tool:
Leaders need to check that each of the attributes is represented in the team.

Using the grid below (or you can decide on your own attributes and qualities) evaluate each member of your team and decide what roles they naturally play in a team situation. With this information, it is easy to deploy your staff appropriately and efficiently.

Name:

Task Roles	Qualities	Rating
Ideas Person	Proposes objectives, ideas, solutions, sets tasks	
Information giver	Gets and offers relevant facts and information	
Information and opinion seeker	Asks for clarification and suggestions, looks for facts and feelings, gets ideas from others, keeps discussion on track	
Co-ordinator	Pulls together ideas, opinion, suggestions. Gives conclusions, moves the group further forward in its pursuit	
Encourager	Supports others, praises and accepts contributions, tries to reduce conflict and tension, opens up opportunities for others to communicate and participate	
Standard setter	Expresses standards that the group should use, reminds group of its aims,	

	keeps discussions from straying	
Implementer	Focused on pragmatics, assimilates ideas and turns them into plans	
Follower	Goes along with the group, accepts ideas of others and willing to compromise for a quiet life	
Blocker	Gets in the way of group progress by getting discussion off topic, focuses on personal issues rather than group task, argues, resists or disagrees often	
Recognition seeker	Tries to get attention, boasts; displays loud or unusual behaviour to call attention to self	

A great tool for encouraging people out of their natural thinking mode is the Six Hats exercise. You will have used the phrase 'lateral thinking' many times. If not, you have certainly heard it used and know exactly what it means. It is part of our everyday lexicon. The man who planted this phrase, and 'thinking out of the box' into our consciousness was Edward de Bono. He also invented the Six Hats as a thought exercise.

"It is unlikely that anyone can really change his character. But it is possible that he can improve the coping

**ability of his character by building on its strong points
rather than trying to overcome the weaknesses."**

Edward de Bono, 1979. "The Happiness Purpose"
Published by Penguin Books

The key point is that a hat is a direction to think rather
than a label for thinking. The key theoretical reasons to use
the Six Thinking Hats are to:

1. encourage Parallel Thinking
2. encourage full-spectrum thinking
3. separate ego from performance

de Bono describes the six hats as a 'game' but you should
be careful not to underestimate the power of its simplicity.
Many major international organisations use this technique for
problem solving.

Each 'hat' represents a perspective or way of thinking.
They are metaphorical hats that a thinker can put on or take
off to indicate the type of thinking they are using.

In a group we can ask members to 'put on' different hats
in a sequence to aid the problem-solving process. The exercise
could even be enhanced by having six actual different
coloured hats, which might even make it a bit more engaging.

Using a sequence can help overcome the problem of each
group member adopting random positions at random times. It
also permits us to control people who insist on sticking to one
perspective (e.g. negative) – we can ask them to assume a
different hat.

Tool: Six Hats exercise

There are two ways to carry out this exercise. I tend to laminate each 'Hat' onto a sheet of paper containing both the illustration and the description.

Method 1

1. Give each participant a specific hat (or laminated sheet). When discussing an agenda item, they have to speak in the mode assigned to them, forgoing any natural tendencies.
2. The hats can be rotated for the next agenda item.

Method 2

1. Place all the hats in the centre of the table
2. When speaking, a contributor has to choose the appropriate hat for their contribution.

Both methods encourage team members to consider their contribution carefully and it forces them to find other ways of considering an issue.

Personally, I prefer to assign hats – even if by rotation. That way, each contributor has to really consider their input.

White Hat thinking – Neutral, Objective

This hat covers facts, figures, information needs and gaps. "I think we need some white hat thinking at this point…" means, "Let's drop the arguments and proposals, and look at the data base."

Red Hat thinking – Emotions and feelings

This covers intuition, feelings and emotions, the essence of our connection to one another. The red hat allows the thinker to put forward an intuition without any need to justify it. "Putting on my red hat, I think this is a terrible proposal." Usually feelings and intuition can only be introduced into a discussion if they are supported by logic. When this happens the feeling is genuine but the logic is spurious. The red hat gives full permission to a thinker to put forward his or her feelings on the subject at that moment.

Black Hat thinking – Cautious and careful

This is the hat of judgment and caution. It is a most valuable hat. It is not in any sense an inferior or negative hat. The black hat is used to point out why a suggestion does or does not fit the facts, the available experience, the system in use, or the policy that is being followed. The black hat must always be logical.

Yellow Hat thinking – Positive and optimistic

This is the logical positive. Why something will work and why it will offer benefits. It can be used in looking forward to the results of some proposed action, but can also be used to find something of value in what has already happened.

Green Hat thinking – creative and innovative

This is the hat of creativity, alternatives, proposals, what is interesting, provocations, considerations and changes.

Blue Hat thinking – Control and process

This is the overview or process control hat. It looks not at the subject itself but at the 'thinking' about the subject. "Putting on my blue hat, I feel we should do some more green hat thinking at this point." In technical terms, the blue hat is concerned with meta-cognition.

Leadership Styles

As you will know from your own experience, there are many leadership styles. Some might say, as many as there are leaders. Whilst it is true to acknowledge that we all bring our personality to the leadership qualities that we display, we can usually fit leadership into several groups based on their overall effect.

Most of us will have come across a list of leadership styles commonly acknowledged. These lists abound on the internet, and can be found as a list of 4, or 6, or 8 and of many other numbers. These are completely arbitrary, notional, minimally helpful, and usually only in the author's head since no leader fits neatly into a definable box. They all start with the categorical title, "The 6 management styles" or "The 8 management styles", etc. Using "The", as if it were fact, as if their list is the encyclopaedia of leadership, the final word in how leaders are and should be.

Leadership styles include the following:

1. **Individualist** – focuses on their own needs and professional advance
2. **Strategist** – understands the structures, staff and cultures in which the organisation operates. Able to concentrate on step-by-step plans to engineer development and change management.
3. **Autocratic** – makes decisions without consulting. The despots in the world of work.
4. **Consultative** – engages the employees in discussion, but makes the final decisions.
5. **Democratic** – involves employees in decision making.
6. **Laissez faire** – guides or advises, but allows staff to govern how things are run. May occasionally exercise

their right to nudge things back on course if necessary.

There are many, many more on countless lists. Some reappear on many lists and some only appear on one.

However, whether you find it useful or not to find a niche to slot into as a leader, there are some features that usually make a good leader. People who have a positive regard for their leaders are those who are empowered, included, valued and challenged. Employees who are left to do their own thing are usually unmotivated, while those who are micromanaged will feel disenfranchised. A happy medium is usually the optimum.

Very early in my professional life, I was once informed by a 'helpful' colleague that the 'feedback sandwich' was the best way to handle reportees (I prefer to avoid using the word 'subordinates' as it is demeaning). You start with praise (so they feel good about the meeting and engage with what you have to say next). Then you give them the negative feedback. (The 'meat' of your sandwich, in this model, is to pummel them and analyse their performance to ensure that they know exactly what went wrong). Then you finish with another positive comment. (This is as if to cheerily pat them on the back and send them on their way, like the good child you need them to be, to perform your bidding for the next challenge). I believe that the net result of this strategy is to leave the employee feeling like they have been punched in the face without really understanding why. Whilst it is important to always find the good in the work that your staff members are doing, this was never going to be my model. I don't work to prescription. I am all about generating understanding (on both sides and in both directions) to create motivation and improvement. Effective communication is key to this important attitude.

> **Story:** Many years ago, I had the responsibility to line manage two youngsters in their very first professional role – a sabbatical post (i.e. just for one year, to be replaced by new workers when the year is done). After every project was completed, we would meet to evaluate the project.
>
> While 'Keith' was happy to listen and keen to get the meeting over with, on the first few occasions 'Ron' would eagerly ask me, "how did we do?" I guess he expected a take home message of accolades and praises on one side, and then a short list of things to improve on the other. He soon came to realise that I was never going to issue him with either.
>
> Instead, I would always answer his question with a question, "how do you think you did?" This would lead into meaningful discussion about success criteria and evaluation. By prompting him to channel his thoughts and lead the analysis, Ron was enabled to be much clearer in his own mind as to how well he did – what went well and what could be improved. He picked up the skills, not only of the work he was carrying out – improving each time – but also of evaluation, of prioritisation, and of communication. All valuable workplace skills.
>
> Recently, Ron heard I was in town and made a point of coming to visit me to thank me for the work I did with him. It is now 15 years since our time together and he was keen to tell me that he had employed all the skills that I had imbued him with in his professional life. He was now a manager himself, utilising those skills and managing staff.

> What he would have realised, if he had stopped to think about it, was that I was merely the facilitator. He did all the learning, and all the professional development. I just gave him the opportunity and the platform to increase his skills and confidence in the job.

My policy is not to tell someone what they should or should not have done. They can work that out for themselves. The best way to improve performance is for the employee to recognise that it needs to improve and how to improve. The manager's job is simply to facilitate the employee gaining that knowledge and guide them towards it.

5. Generational Differences

We all know that managers can be different. We've all succumbed to the charms of a manager, or quivered under the despotism of another. However, not many of us stop to consider that our colleagues, born in different eras, are culturally different to us.

Language changes, ethics change, attitudes change, expectations change ... In addition, the way we perform our jobs is completely different for each generation.

Below are a few pencil sketches of the various generations and what their era might mean for the workplace. These are by no means across the board for all individuals, but it is helpful to examine how the conditions and environment of the era people are born in can shape how they approach their work.

GI Generation (born 1900–1924)

I don't imagine many of us would be still working with a GI generationer, but worth starting here as we will have known these individuals. They lived through the war years (maybe even both wars), and experienced the great depression. Generally, their young working lives were beset with hardships. As such, the GI Generation were happy making do – fixing rather than replacing, making ends meet by cutting corners or innovating ways of working, and generally being amenable to altruistically working long hours in poor conditions to ensure the company's success. They experienced dramatic rise in living standards through their lives. They were strait-laced rule followers who achieved a great deal in virtually every sphere of life. They were civic minded and community spirited, leading to their loyalty to their workplace and supportive attitude towards colleagues. Interestingly, in their youth, the term "teenager" was not in use, nor was it recognised as a phase. People went from being children to becoming adults. It was only with the advent of economic growth that children had the luxury of enjoying life before becoming responsible adults.

Silent Generation (born 1925–1945)

"Children should be seen and not heard." The parents of these children were often working hard on the war effort, leaving their youngsters to play with each other in the street or to sit quietly and "mind their manners". Their work life was about making plans for the future. They married and had families younger than any of the other generations before or since. They missed out on their teenage years, becoming adults straight from childhood. They were lucky to come of age in a booming economy. They were a small cohort due to low birth-rates, so they had the pick of the crop in terms of the labour market. As a result, they earned well and were happy with their work/life balance, and the measures taken to retain them in the workplace. In Britain, the Silents had access to the new National Health Service, free medical and health treatment at the point of use. This meant that they didn't have to save for their medical bills, but could spend on other lifestyle fripperies. This made for an affluent generation. By their late adulthoods, this generation were better off than their parents had been and retired comfortably.

Baby Boomers (born 1946–1964)

Born directly after WWII, Baby Boomers benefitted from a growing economy. They grew up in an age where their work was providing good benefits – both financial and social. Knowing that there are rewards for their hard work can make Baby Boomers quite competitive and goal orientated. They are also a much larger cohort than the Silent Generation, so competition in the workplace has been necessary for them. Since there is competition for their jobs, they tend to play by the rules, and have a good work ethic. They work by the adage that coming late to a meeting is a message that your time is more important than the people you are meeting. They just don't do it. They arrive at work on time, are diligent and hard working. They always meet deadlines and stick strictly to budgets.

Generation X (born 1965–1979)

Gen Xers arose on the tails of the Baby Boomers. They saw the fall of some great world orders such as Communist Europe and Apartheid South Africa; they were children when the Vietnam war defined the era. They entered adulthood as the world became technology focused. Mobile phones were being developed, the Internet was taking off, and the advent of social media all shaped how this generation used their leisure time, and how they entered the professional world. As kids, this was the first generation where it was the norm for both parents to go out to work. This is the 'me' generation. Gen Xers, unlike their predecessors, are not focused on the future – theirs or the geopolitical planet's, but on their own and their children's present stability.

Millennials (born 1980–2000), Sometimes Called Generation Y

Millennials grew up with the Internet, with technology and with a fast-evolving rate of technological development. They have access to TV, movies and information from anywhere in the world. This makes them more culturally savvy too. Increased international migration adds to their cultural adaptation. Access to the Internet has made them more morally grounded as well as knowledgeable. They are the generation who balked at single-use plastics, rejected the use of animals for human entertainment and attire, outed predatory males in the #MeToo movement. In the workplace, they will seek sound moral systems and practices, but they are also self-obsessed. Gone are the days of the GI generation where workers did their bosses' bidding. Millennials expect to be consulted democratically, and they expect their welfare needs to be met before those of the company.

Generation Z (born 2000–Present)

Gen Z are just entering the workplace. They have grown up fully technologically literate. They have never known the non-smart mobile phones of old, let alone a landline phone. They grew up with information at their fingertips on their

Smartphones. They will have no patience with poor research or poorly presented data. They can check on the veracity of any information in seconds. Their work ethic is likely to be predicated on the expectation to be able to work flexibly, and at home at least some of the time.

Exercise:

1. Divide your team into groups or pairs.
2. Assign each group with a generation.
3. Each group researches their particular generation's attributes and qualities.
4. Each group produces an advertising campaign specifically targeted at their assigned generation.
5. Share in plenum

Language

As well as attitudes, technology and work ethic, it may be worthwhile to remember that language changes dramatically as well. If it didn't, we would all be speaking Chaucerian English, Anglo Saxon dialects of our forebears or maybe even ancient Aramaic as spoken in biblical times. Language is evolving particularly fast in the last 150 years. Even a few decades has made a huge difference to the way we speak. Take the hippie era expressions "far out", "groovy" etc. and compare it with today's words such as "epic", "YOLO". Unintelligible in the respective opposite eras. Then there are the words that mean the opposite of what we might imagine. "Sick" means fantastic, for instance. There are words that have lost their original meaning. "Awesome", when I was growing up was reserved for the likes of moon travel, extreme acts of God, or really influential relationships. Today, it simply means anything that is quite good. "That dessert was awesome."

Portmanteau words such as "bromance" and "ginormous" would have been unknown to our parents. "Cool" is a generic term for "nice", "great", "that's okay", "I approve" or any number of positive proclamations. Although around in America for many decades, "cool" only started to permeate British society in the last 30 years or so.

With the increasing use of mobile phones and texting, younger generations are creating shortcuts and acronyms which have entered our lexicon as new words. For instance, LOL, which stands for laughing out loud, conveys a response to a comment that the person on the other end of the conversation will appreciate. Nowadays, youngsters can be heard to say "lol" to each other in face-to-face conversation. In fact, I have heard of older folk thinking it stood for "Lots of Love" and texting it to relatives in the event of a bereavement. Such is the miscommunication across the generations.

Generations who hadn't experienced each other's era would have been completely bemused, at best. Time travel couldn't ever be clandestine because a time traveller would stick out like a sore thumb by the language they use – even in a matter of decades.

Where there is a workplace with mixed generations, it is important to recognise that people may not mean what you think they do.

Workplace Expectations

Younger generations have grown up with an attitude of caution. Health and Safety was not a "thing" when I entered the work place. We took our chances with whatever environment we entered, and no-one sued anyone if the air-conditioning broke and they suffered an asthma attack. We just accepted some of the risks of what we did. Nowadays, when starting a new job, the Human Resources department arranges for an assessment of ergonomic seating, appropriate lighting, suitable ventilation and so on. In addition to an entirely healthy work environment, Millennials will also expect time off for medical, dental and optical appointments during their working day. This was unheard of in the generations that preceded them, who would arrange their appointments in their time off.

6. Qualities of a Good Leader

"The greatest leader is not necessarily the one who does the greatest things. He is the one that gets the people to do the greatest things."

Ronald Reagan

"As we look ahead into the next century, leaders will be those who empower others."

Bill Gates

Both Ronald Reagan and Bill Gates are saying the same thing. Lead from behind. I always liken leadership to the heat in a percolator. The leader is at the bottom pushing the team members upwards – towards exposure and production.

> **Exercise:**
>
> 1. Think of a person you like or admire. Any person; doesn't have to be work related.
> 2. On a scale of 1 to 10, how much do you trust this person?
> 3. On a scale of 1 to 10, how much do you respect this person?
> 4. Multiply these numbers together. This number needs to be over 75.
>
> Be that person!

We all instinctively know what a good leader is like. They make you feel good about the work that you are doing; they encourage you; they challenge you just enough to push your boundaries and enable you to pick up new skills; and they generally enhance both your enjoyment for the job and your professional experience.

Encouragement

A good manager will remind you about your previous success, praise you regularly for work done well, and check in frequently with you to offer praise and invite queries. These check-ins should never be used for micro-management, but instead as a means of reminding you that you are part of a team and your work is valued.

Poor managers are easier to spot and it is not worth enumerating their qualities or techniques. Neither is it worth listing the qualities of a good manager. We all know one when we see one.

Story: I once had a colleague (let's call her Sally) whose line manager (Michael) was very good at his job, accomplished in his performance and generally well-liked in the organisation – both by colleagues and stakeholders. However, despite being in his late 50s, this was his first management position and he struggled with the concept, and really didn't know how to manage another individual. It seemed that his view of line management was to issue directives and closely monitor the work. There was never praise and never a check that all was well.

One example of this attitude was when, on their weekly catch-up meeting, Sally explained that later that day she had a visiting speaker coming to give a talk to one of their stakeholder regional branches. The speaker had brought her own projection equipment but the screen was damaged and beyond use. The branch didn't have one of their own. Obviously, Sally intended to source a screen for the event and had no qualms about her ability to do so in time for the event.

Michael then began a long, detailed directive instructing her who to phone to get them to bring a screen (people not even in the organisation), how to transport it, what favours to reign in, how to persuade the person to bring it over … and so on.

This conversation left Sally feeling untrusted, micro-managed and undervalued. She knew exactly where to access a screen and was confident that it would be in situ by the time of the talk. It was a trivial matter that he really didn't need to be involved in as her line-manager.

Had he first enquired whether she needed assistance or if she was confident in performing this small task, both Sally and Michael would have felt better about the

> manager/reportee interaction, and her ability to do her job confidently. Instead, he wasted time in giving her unnecessary directives, undermined her capabilities and demotivated her.

Motivation

We often think that it is money that motivates people. Give them a raise and they will perform better, or not seek another job. Actually, it's not money at all. The things that motivate us most of all are recognition, connection and authenticity.

Research by Festinger in 1957 into Cognitive Dissonance found that the higher the financial incentives, the worse we perform. The understanding behind this is that we value the work more if it has less financial incentive because we feel that the value is in the work itself rather than the remuneration.

Consider these things which you can easily do to demonstrate these attitudes:

1. First, do no harm (and, if you can't remember any other, remember this one)
2. Treat them well
3. Give them a purpose
4. Make the work dignified (so, in the above example, don't include borrowing a screen as a work directive). Ensure that they have autonomy and mastery over their work.

This will lead to better performance and more satisfaction, both of which are innate motivators themselves. It becomes a vicious circle (or a virtuous circle if you are a millennial).

On the flipside is my story about Jane who had just been given new management responsibility. However, this promotion was based on the work she had done thus far, and she was given no training to perform her new responsibilities.

Story

Jane worked for a charity. On being promoted, she was asked to keep track of the donor records. On one occasion, she was asked to remove all the donors from the spreadsheet who were no longer donating to the organisation.

Taking the initiative (which is why she was given the promotion in the first place), she decided to not fully delete these people, but simply to strike through their names on the spreadsheet so that colleagues could still access information about them in the future, should they wish to.

When her line manager saw what she had done, she castigated her rather severely for leaving sensitive information on the system when it should have been deleted.

Had she given Jane clear instructions, or trained her in the proper way to handle donor information, Jane would have had no problem following those instructions. Instead, she was left to her own devices in the new role, and managers assumed that she knew what she was doing.

The result was that now Jane was trepidatious about approaching her manager for support when she needed it, scared of a reproach and worried about giving the wrong impression of her abilities.

With autonomy, therefore, needs to be motivation. We need to know why we are performing a task, and not just

---

doing someone's bidding. Understanding what we are doing results in more agency and improved performance.

We always give induction training to new staff but we tend to forget to give interim training to staff who move up, or across, the organisation. This reminds me of the Peter Principle, that we rise to our level of incompetence. In other words, we do well and get promoted, but then we are out of our depth. It doesn't have to be this way if only we paid attention to the continued professional development of our up-and-coming staff.

Help

We all need assistance or guidance at one time or another. Especially in a job where you may be picking up new skills or learning new systems. A good leader will be able to take you through these learning experiences in a positive way, and be available to guide you when you need advice.

A good leader will help you.

A good leader will start by showing you how to do something or demonstrate how it works. They will check that you can do it and then walk away and let you discover the intricacies and nuances of the system for yourself. Overbearing managers will correct you at every turn, giving you no space to discover for yourself or to make mistakes which will enhance your learning.

The reverse can also be true. I have come across far too many people who have told me that their manager gave them the outline of the job when they first joined the company, but then never checked up on them to make sure that they were happy in the job, doing what they are supposed to be doing, or checking that the work being done matched up to managerial expectations.

It's about expectation. If the employee knows that the manager expects them to shine, they will. If the manager conveys that they have no expectations or that they expect the employee to do badly, then they are demotivating the employee and giving them no goals to achieve.

Instead of giving information, a good manager will give reading material or starter references. Through following these, an employee should be able to formulate a good knowledge of the subject, develop a sense of the pros and cons, and can argue the case should it be necessary. Without doing their own research, an employee will just be repeating what they have been told or, worse, having to follow something that they don't believe in.

If people have a strong belief system (for example, how things are, or should be, done) you could give them the facts, but this will just cause them to formulate a stronger argument to support their belief. "Inoculation Theory" suggests that you expose people to a weak form of the misinformation. They will then formulate an argument to refute it. This works in much the same way as a real inoculation encourages the body to mount an immune response to a viral invasion when first confronted with a weakened form of it.

Thus, the best way to engender a solid grounding in an area of information is to 'inoculate' someone with a weak argument, to which they are forced to make a considered counter-argument. If a set of values is to be adopted, cognitive support for them has to be developed. Such cognitive support makes one resistant to counterargument persuasion. The strength of an attitude or belief is based, in part, on the degree of thinking the person has done about it.

The best leaders show confidence in their team by leaving them to get on with it. However, they also make themselves available for guidance, discussion or questions. A manager who is not available to answer questions will be seen as aloof, supercilious or contemptuous.

An individual who is floundering will be left feeling demotivated, frustrated and disloyal if their manager is not available to keep them going in the right direction with their project.

A leader who does none of the things mentioned above (demonstrates, guides, answers questions) leaves their team members feeling frustrated, unmotivated, hurt, lost and even depressed.

Jane, from the story above, told me that she was very lucky when she entered the organisation to have the best manager in the organisation. She had a comprehensive induction, including how to do things, who to approach for what and even the style guide. However, she observed that some of her colleagues who started at the same time as her didn't have as good an induction and didn't know many of the things that Jane was taught when she entered the organisation. How simple it would have been for managers to get together to formulate a comprehensive induction for all incoming staff.

Story:

Sophie had a new job in a large national public body. She was to be a research manager. She had been a researcher before, but had never managed research conducted by others. She had to be taught the system. The research 'question' usually arises from another sector or from outside bodies. Her job is to decide whether it warrants being conducted, put out a tender for a team to do the research, lead the team in what is expected and establish the null hypothesis, and then wait for the research to be done for her to read and edit the report.

She found this frustrating. From being a researcher in the field, she was suddenly a pen-pusher. She had no idea how to do the things she needed to do. She attended meetings where the language was completely mystifying. For instance, 'comms' kept coming up and she had no idea what it meant. She didn't know where or how to tender. Didn't know how to select the best research team, what were the criteria to use for this decision.

Occasionally, she would be given a piece of editing of a report, or evaluating a research project. Here she shone, but it was easy work that was beneath what she was supposed to be doing. Often, she would hide away in one of these editing projects, knowing that she was being productive – even though it was not the main focus of the work she should have been doing. She still fundamentally didn't know how to do her job.

The problem was in the nature of the organisation. It had three centres. Her line manager was elsewhere. Sophie was assigned local colleagues, equal to her in the hierarchy, to ask for advice or clarity. When she did approach them for advice, she found that they were too busy trying to ensure that they were producing good work within their deadlines, to focus on Sophie and her plight. The team manager would arrive fortnightly and conduct meetings or training with the local team. This still left Sophie behind. She still didn't know what 'comms' meant (or many of the other esotericisms of working language, policy or protocol) and the esoteric language seemed central to what was going on.

Sophie ended up leaving after just three months. She tried to leave after six weeks but her line manager persuaded her to stay on the basis that he would be there for her and support her a little more. He wasn't and didn't.

She became more and more depressed, her sleep suffered as she tried to make sense of what she was doing, and her self-esteem plummeted as she increasingly realised that she was useless in her job.

Bob was a great manager, but he just wasn't there. Sophie was a great researcher and employee, but no-one showed her how to do her job.

What this story relates is that without a line manager who is on hand to demonstrate, give direction or support, a new worker, however dedicated and experienced, cannot do their job properly.

> **Challenge:**
>
> Identify five things you could have implemented to ease Sophie into the position and ensure that she was effective in her job, and that her line manager was approachable and instructional.
>
> 1. _____
> 2. _____
> 3. _____
> 4. _____
> 5. _____

Some of my suggestions would be as follows:

1. Ensure that her induction includes a **visit to the branch where her line manager works**. This will give her a sound idea of how things get done there, what sort of times the manager is available to take calls, and how amenable the manager is to answering colleagues' questions. It also establishes a solid relationship between Sophie and her line manager.

2. Give her a dedicated person in her local office **whose job it is to oversee** her integration into the work. Not just colleagues who she can turn to, but a person who takes an interest in what she is doing and who is invested in her doing the job well.

3. Ensure that she is **trained in language** and location. A quick lexicon of words and phrases that she might encounter would have enabled her to be up to speed very quickly. We all use jargon and organisation specific acronyms. They may seem obvious to those

working there, but to a newcomer, they are a complete mystery and, indeed, they serve to mystify the work itself. Understanding that 'comms' is the communications department, and where they are would help her to approach them when needed.

4. For those pieces she was enjoying editing, someone could have explained how the project had come this far. A **step-by-step guide leading to something she was familiar with** (i.e., the piece she was editing) would have been very meaningful contextualised in a project she had become familiar with. It would have made it much easier for her to understand the procedure than just being given the theoretical process.

5. Include a period of **shadowing** one of her colleagues through the entire process. This way she can ask questions as issues arise and she can learn the process first hand in a real project, being in the presence of someone experienced at doing what she has to learn to do.

6. Make sure that a **regular timely catch up** is scheduled for Sophie to communicate with the line-manager over the phone or Zoom. This could be daily, or weekly (please, not less often). Make sure it is not confrontational or asking her to report. It is about opening up the space for her to express her reservations and concerns. A truly open conversation will turn these anxieties into learning.

7. Language

I was once a regional director in a charitable organisation where the CEO used to refer to the premises of the organisation as "my campus" and to the organisation itself as "my institute". Nobody wants to work for someone like that, to be someone's servant. We need to feel that we are part of something, that our voice and our actions make a difference to the organisation. We need to feel that we are serving a community, not some despot sitting in a central office who has two secretaries and has everything done for him.

The language we use makes a huge difference, not only to our understanding of the work and its projects but to the nature of how we are regarded and the agency we have in our own work. Had this CEO referred to 'our' instead of 'my', he would have been including the staff and demonstrating a value in their work. Not only that, but by using terms such as 'our', he would be encouraging an emotional investment. His chosen language demonstrated a sense of superiority. We were his minions. Even 'the' organisation would have identified the institute as something we can all focus on. Rather than him being at the centre, the work that we do with 'the' organisation is central, even if we are not.

Exercise:

1. Identify a real problem or issue that currently needs addressing in your organisation.
2. Give it a title.
3. Write a brief blurb that you will use to introduce it to the staff at the next staff meeting. Don't think; just get it down on paper as quickly as you can.
4. Now look at your written piece and edit it to be as inclusive and encouraging to the staff as you can. Make the staff central. Use words such as 'we' and 'us'. And use language that encourages the staff to be involved, in fact, language that engages them and motivates them entirely as owners of the issue, and that unites them as a team.

Nobody bonds over deadlines; they bond over camaraderie and shared experiences.

Another focus on language should be to create possibility. Use creative words rather than specific ones. For instance, "could" instead of "should"; "possibly" instead of "definitely"; "maybe", to introduce a topic, and so on. By opening up possibilities, staff become part of the solution and know that there is not a definitive answer that they have to find. So many teachers, trainers and bosses use what I call the "what's-in-my-head" type of question. This creates a failure situation when those being asked don't get it "right". Create a situation where there is no right or wrong. Imbue the staff with ownership and opportunities.

Questions

Even if you have never had a baby, you will know one thing about babies. They cry. We also know that they cry for a reason. There are only three reasons that babies cry: They are hungry or thirsty, they need a nappy change, they are in pain or discomfort. They can't talk yet so it is the carer's job to interrogate the situation.

- Do they need feeding?
- Do they need changing?
- Are they hot, cold, in pain …?

This response is instinctive. You want the crying to stop so you work out what is making it happen.

As the baby grows into a child, we start to forget that instinct. Toddlers and children try to express their concerns before resorting to crying. They speak to you using their still developing language and communication skills. When that doesn't work, they express their frustrations in other ways to get your attention. They may become violent, disobedient, insolent ... or a host of other behaviours that are undesirable. What do most parents do? They punish the behaviour, discipline the child or remonstrate with them. In their frustration, parents forget how to interrogate the situation, find out what is behind the behaviour, investigate what will make the child happy.

Even more so, when we go on to become colleagues and leaders. We forget that employees are disgruntled for a reason. People often approach leaders for answers, but in reality, the leaders don't always have the answers and begin to give spontaneous answers because they have been put on the spot.

Turn it around.

You know what the problem is.

- Disgruntled employees
- Poor performance
- Poor staff relationships

Now try and work out what will solve it. Don't rebuke. Find out how to resolve the situation.

There are so many ways to ask questions. Sometimes a direct question can seem confrontational. At other times, the absence of a question might seem uncaring. Use your professional judgement as to which applies in your situation.

Whatever your style, it is important to hear those answers regularly. As a leader, you need to let your team members know that you care, that they matter, and that their perspective is invaluable. On a weekly basis, finding the time to have one-to-one meetings with each of your staff members is invaluable. If you are in a large organisation and it is logistically impossible, then establish a cascade system of managers talking to their staff, and reporting back up to their line managers.

Questions that should be addressed weekly should include:

1. How are you feeling?
2. What is going well?
3. What would you like to improve?
4. What can we do to make you feel more fulfilled?
5. What would you like me to know? How can I be a better leader?

And here's the background to those questions.

1. How are you feeling?

   1. It's all very well to say that you should leave your personal life at home. But a depressed employee is a depressed employee, regardless of the source of their feeling low. It helps to know how our staff are so that we can ameliorate their negative feelings. Someone wallowing in grief, might just appreciate some friendly chats; conversely, they might feel that their colleagues are being intrusive and want to isolate from the milieu for a bit; or their particular project might be a bit triggering and it would help to move to something else temporarily. Whatever the issues, knowing how your team are feeling will help to ensure that you can put things in place to improve their wellbeing if necessary

2. What is going well?

   2. Success is the best motivator there can possibly be. If the individual is given a platform to sing their own praises, this can be extremely reinforcing and rewarding. If the staff member identifies something that they excel at, give them more of that type of work to do.

3. What would you like to improve?

   3. Not only does it give you, the manager, an inkling of where support will be necessary or training need to be implemented, but it gives the staff member an opportunity to evaluate their own performance and recognise improvements to be made. It also gives them a chance to tell you that they know, and that they are striving to do better. They don't need to be admonished.

4. What can we do to make you feel more fulfilled?
   4. Shows that you care about the employee and is a very good way to make effective improvements in the work environment, and to respond directly to their requests, which will pay dividends in productivity.

5.   What would you like me to know? How can I be a better leader?

   5.   This places you as an empathetic leader, someone who is approachable and amenable to change, and is a great starting point for self-development. It also helps you to assimilate the facts on the ground – those things that the staff are all muttering about to each other. These are often things that are very easy to change, had you known about them.

8. Meetings

"If I am not for myself, who will be for me? And if I am only for myself, what am 'I'?"

Hillel

If I were to ask you, "what is the purpose of meetings?" what would your answer be? Go on. Make a bullet pointed list.

1. _____
2. _____
3. _____
4. _____
5. _____
6. _____

The chances are that somewhere on your list would be one or more of these:

- information dissemination
- instruction
- motivation
- sharing of calendars

- announcing achievements

A random internet search on management skills suggests the following (with my comments in brackets) as reasons for meetings.

1. **Pool and develop ideas** (Seriously?! Nobody is listening to anybody else; They are just waiting their turn to have their say).
2. **Plan** (Really?! We need a meeting for that? We all know that the team leader issues directives and we follow them).
3. **Solve problems** (Right! Like problems are always solved by assembling the staff to discuss it ad nauseum. Remember, we should be focussing on **solutions**, not problems).
4. **Make decisions** (Well, if sending a member of the team away to investigate is a decision …)
5. **Create and develop understanding** (Understanding is rarely generated by an assembly of people; it takes research, motivation and involvement to engender understanding).
6. **Encourage enthusiasm and initiative** (Oh! Is that what the cake and doughnuts were for?!)
7. **Provide a sense of direction** (As dictated by the meeting chair)
8. **Create a common purpose** (Are purpose and direction not the same thing? You see, just more waffle and waste of time).

Some of these are on my own list above, but in more florid language (e.g. instructions become "provide a sense of direction"; sharing calendars becomes "Plan", and so on). And I do believe that this list is a true reflection of what most meetings are about.

Have a look at the list you created and at the two above. How many of those items could not be achieved by use of a memo or e-mail exchange? Honestly.

This is not to say that I believe that meetings have no place. They do. But their purpose in my view is not about creating plans around an agenda. I think they play a much more important role. Meetings, if conducted well, should promote collaboration and co-operation. Feeling part of a team and feeling that everyone's work is being recognised is vital in ensuring that every member of the team is working at their optimal. Anything less is demoralising.

Meetings function to combine and synergise skills. It is only when all members of the team are assembled that new alliances can be made between participants. When two people with completely different skills come together to look at an issue, amazing innovations can result. Each brings a different perspective and understanding.

By the same token, ideas can be piggy-backed. Sometimes an idea can trigger a thought in someone else and the initial idea can be reified much more readily.

Relationships are often forged in meetings. If everyone is working in their silos, nobody gets the social benefits of working in a team. Meetings fulfil the necessity for social interaction which results in better working conditions, synergistic problem solving and mutual support.

Most meetings are about the convenor having a firm idea of what needs to be achieved, and they steer the meeting in the desired direction. Differences of opinion are politely heard, but rarely incorporated. People are encouraged to have their say, but the end of the meeting is about agreeing with what the boss wants to happen.

The great Jewish leader and sage from the 1st century BC, Hillel, was famous for his sayings, "If I am not for myself, who will be for me? And if I am only for myself, what am 'I'?" These are pertinent here. Meetings are not about you, the employee, or even about you, the manager. They are about the team. They are about each person representing themselves effectively, but also about each member giving full credibility to every other member of the team. This is what creates collaboration and mutual respect, and achieves goals.

There was a much more interesting and relevant story that Hillel is also famous for. The story goes that a prospective convert to Judaism went to several sages and asked to be taught everything he needs in order to be accepted into the faith. He was impatient and demanded that the sages give him the entire scripture in condensed form – while he stood on one leg, to ensure brevity and succinctness. After he was rejected by several teachers, Hillel accepted the challenge. His lesson: "What is hateful to you, do not do to your neighbour. That is the whole Torah; the rest is the commentary – go and study it!"

Perhaps we should be demanding that our managers and team leaders give us the information we need while we stand on one leg. How much more efficient would our workplace be? What we need to know needs to be studied. It can't be relayed in summary. We all know that we gained our most knowledge and understanding in the job in the first few months of **doing** it. Nothing can be taught that needs to be experienced. Indeed, we gained even more understanding once we had to teach it to someone else.

The point to be made here is not that everything can be distilled into a short strapline, but that the essence is in the study, the buy-in, the motivation, the effort.

Let's find ways of making meetings meaningful. Meaningful means that people come away with buy-in, come away wanting to be a part of the project and come away as part of a productive team, with a clear role which dovetails with the other roles.

One effective way of involving the team in a productive meeting is the "Four Part Meeting".

1.   The Connection Phase

Make sure that you connect to:

- The content
- The processes
- The team members

Ensure that all present are fully aware of the content, and that the process is connected to you as the chair. This means that it will serve you well to check on this at the start of the meeting – assuming that you have disseminated all of the relevant documentation such as agenda, minutes of the last meeting, background reading and so on.

Instead of making the agenda the starting point, perhaps a round table discussion about what needs to happen and where you are up to would be much more helpful. This serves many purposes: it helps to focus minds on the true issues, reminds participants where they got up to with the ongoing discussion, and why it needs to be resolved. It involves everyone in creating the agenda and agreeing that it is appropriate.

2.   Activation Phase

Make it interesting! We have all sat in meetings where people drone on and on. Everyone seems to want to take a turn at saying what's already been said, and nothing of value is achieved.

There are many ways to hold colleagues' attention in a meeting. For instance, use a variety of presentation techniques, call on different people to present different aspects, set challenges or pose questions. All of these promote collaboration, maintain attention, and enhance sharing of information.

There are many ideas for checking in with the team to see what people think or what they already understand about the problem. Here are just a few. They are quick, snappy and fun ideas to liven up the meeting, promote discussion and demonstrate existing knowledge. They all seem facile at first glance, but they all promote engagement.

- Writing on a post-it (what they already know/want to know; questions; success criteria etc) and post on a board for all to share. Then assemble Post-it note ideas into groups.
- Card sort. Ordinate ideas into levels of importance, collection of skills needed, information to be learned

or anything else that would benefit from being assembled in order.

- Odd-one-out. A quick snappy way to analyse what needs to be concentrated on.
- Use a picture/object/short written source/video clip etc. as initial stimulus material to lead team members to the meeting's desired objective(s)/outcome(s).
- Key word and definition matching. This ensures that the team are focusing on a shared understanding.
- Envelopes on the table (containing brain teasers, puzzles or conundrums on the topic) Pairs each grab one and complete the puzzles and then present their findings to the group.
- Brainstorm/mind map/labelling/drawing.
- Using an anecdote to personalise the abstract.
- Think-pair-share discussion about a specific topic/question. This means think as an individual, pair up with another member of the team to discuss your respective ideas, and then share in plenum the agreed points.

3. Demonstrate Phase

Give colleagues a clear opportunity to demonstrate that they have taken the issue/s on board. This can be done in many ways. For instance,

- go around the room asking each person to suggest the next action on the list
- pair up and discuss what each person's understanding is

- divide into small groups, each creating a quick presentation.

4. Consolidation Phase

Allow Colleagues to reflect on the content of the meeting and agree the process.

1. Summarise, linking to the key concepts of big picture
2. Agree on success criteria for the project
3. Agree on roles for the different aspects of the project

Exercise:

1. Create an agenda that is relevant to your work

_____

_____

_____

_____

_____

2. How will you ensure that all delegates are au fait with what the meeting is about? List all of the ways that you can think of that this could be done.

_____

_____

_____

_____

_____

---

3. What means will you use to keep it interesting? List as many as you can. Remember the individuals in your team and try to create focus that would be interesting for each of them.

_____

_____

_____

_____

_____

4. What techniques will you employ for team members to demonstrate their understanding?

_____

_____

_____

_____

_____

9. Communication

Communication, from the word, commune (together), means sharing and exchanging information or ideas between people, and includes verbal, nonverbal, written and visual.

There are many reasons why we communicate. These include:

1. Exchange or impart information
2. Instruct
3. Consolidate knowledge
4. Guide
5. Warn
6. Discuss
7. Persuade
8. Debate
9. Clarification

Verbal

Communication is the grease that smooths relationships. However, it is also vital for instruction, debate and information sharing in the workplace.

Meetings are a classic example of good use of verbal communication. It is important to have meetings so that ideas are exchanged, information is imparted and discussion can be conducted to arrive at a plan of action. However, all too often meetings are called as a formality. They generate a lot of discussion, but nothing is planned. Meetings should be on point, necessary and productive. If they don't serve a purpose (other than getting the team together), they should be dispensed with.

Written

My main focus is the written communication we carry out in the workplace.

Story:

Gemma worked as a manager in a regional office of a multi-centred NFP. When she first started, she was bewildered by packages that used to arrive in the post from the HR department in the headquarters. She would receive HR magazines with a page number on a note. No further instructions or clarification of what she was receiving and why. It would arrive in a brown envelope with a list of all the people to which it had to be circulated. There were signatures next to some of the names. She soon realised that she was being asked to read the articles, sign that she had done so, and then send them on to another person on the list who had not yet signed.

Gemma wasn't in HR and the articles were rarely helpful or instructional for her line of work.

It was never explained to her why she was receiving these, or what help they would be in her work. She got to a point where she would receive the package, dutifully sign, and then pass on to the next person.

No-one had advised Gemma that these packages were going to arrive, nor what to do with them. She had to work it out for herself. Most importantly, no-one had communicated with her enough to motivate her to read these articles.

This story is a classic example of very poor organisational communication. Had the HR Director advised her of the impending arrival of these packages, and why they were being sent out, Gemma would have understood what her task was, and why it was important. Perhaps a covering note with a reason why the HR Director thought it was important to the work that the organisation was doing would have gone a long way to motivating the managers to read it.

Another example of poor communication that people have described to me is the custom of organisational leaders (or sometimes employees) sending out e-mails cc'd to an entire organisation, when it really only affects a handful of individuals. What then ensues is multiple to-and-fro exchanges between the relevant handful. These have to be opened, read and discarded. A huge waste of time for the workforce. Multiply that by the number of people having to do that and we can get a substantial number of person-hours wasted. We forget, when sending these mass mail-outs, that the recipients need to open and read them to decide that they are not relevant. We can't always judge that by the sender or the subject matter.

Non-Verbal

There is also another facet to communication; that of the non-verbal cues. We are leaking information all the time about how we are feeling, what we are thinking or what our innate reactions are to what we are being told. For instance, a shy person coming into a new job may bow their head, hunch their shoulders and not make eye contact. These are all things that we can actively work on regardless of how we are feeling. The following are the elements that we can learn to control to change the perception that people have of us.

1. **Voice.** The cadence, volume, tone and expression that we use can all be modulated to give the message that we wish to convey about ourselves.

2. **Body language.** The way we move, our deportment, or the way we hold our head up will give many messages about who we are and what we are conveying. Dress also comes into this. In the workplace, we are much more inclined to look favourably on someone who is dressed professionally than someone in shorts and a t-shirt, for instance.

3. **Hands.** The way we use our hands when talking can tell a lot. Politicians are taught not to point, so you will often see them holding up a thumb and a forefinger pressed together when stressing a point. If we are fidgeting or twiddling our thumbs when listening, it tells your speaker that you are not interested and are finding ways to pass the time. Whether this is true or not, it's best to avoid giving that message.

4. **Eye contact.** Avoiding eye contact makes you look shifty and untrustworthy, or gives the impression that you have something to hide. Making eye contact shows that you are listening and taking an interest.

5. **Confidence.** Even if you are feeling really nervous, shy or apprehensive, the best way to avoid leaking that information is to act confident. Here is an example where the adage "fake it until you make it" really holds true. If you portray yourself as having confidence – head up, shoulders back, confident stride with large steps, make eye contact, firm

handshake, open body posture, speak clearly – the confidence will follow.

Visual

Visual communication is usually things like street signs and semaphore, neither of which should concern us in the workplace. However, it also includes the signage around the building.

All too often signs are randomly placed around the building with little regard to aesthetics. Not that signs are used for aesthetic purposes, but if they are clustered together, all posted on top of each other, out-of-date or just poorly constructed, they will not be noticed or read.

It is important to keep the posters and announcements area neat, uncluttered and relevant. Old and outdated notices should be regularly discarded. People will then notice when there is a new post and will be more inclined to read it.

The other thing that we find in workplace notices is that they often tend to be negative and give an unpleasant message to users of the space. So, things like, "don't leave your printed material here" by the photocopier, "don't leave your dirty cups in the sink" in the kitchen area, "don't sit on the blue seats" and so on. They leave people feeling that there are a lot of proscribed activities and it creates an unpleasant environment. If we turn these notices around, we can brighten the mood of our employees. Best not to have too many notices at all, but, if you must, how about changing the above to "remember to take your photocopies", "please wash your cups" or the "blue seating area is for visitors". Just avoid the "don't" notices.

Active Listening

Martin Buber, the Austrian philosopher suggested that there are three types of dialogue:

1. *There is genuine dialogue – no matter whether spoken or silent – where each of the participants really has in mind the other or others in their present and particular being and turns to them with the intention of establishing a living mutual relation between himself and them.*
2. *There is technical dialogue, which is prompted solely by the need of objective understanding.*
3. *And there is monologue disguised as dialogue, in which two or more men, meeting in space, speak each with himself in strangely tortuous and circuitous ways and yet imagine they have escaped the torment of being thrown back on their own resources.*

Buber 1947

The first is what we should be striving for in all of our interactions, a conversation where both or all parties are listening to what the others have to say, and only speaking to add to the conversation or to respond to what they have heard. They listen to what others are saying and take it on board before entering with their own thoughts.

The other two are all too familiar, unfortunately. Technical dialogue is what often happens in the workplace. Someone needs to show you how things are done, how something works or similar. The only reason that the listener needs to speak is to either verify understanding or ask questions to enhance understanding.

Monologue disguised as dialogue is, unfortunately, what most of us do most of the time. You know that conversation you are having; someone is regaling you with an interesting/amusing tale, and you wait for a gap in the account so that you can tell your similar tale. We each take it in turns to say something related to the last, but entirely our own story, and moving on from the last story.

Real dialogue happens when you listen to the speaker and then interrogate their account. This might just be the usual how, what, where, when type of response but it might equally be more probing such as "how were you feeling?", "what made you do/say that?" etc. This is real dialogue. You have listened to the story and want to engage with the story.

So here are the key points to remember when trying to engage in genuine dialogue:

1. When appropriate paraphrase and ask appropriate questions. Engage with what the speaker is saying and reflect it back to them. Do not add your own anecdote related to what they have just said.
2. Suspend all extraneous thoughts – including any additions you might make to the conversation.
3. Nod or shake your head at the appropriate junctures, and make eye contact. Use empathetic facial expressions.

I once learned a useful acronym for communication when the other party is arguing with you. ESP. Listen to what they have to say and then:

1. Explain what you have understood their position to be.
2. Sympathise with their take on the situation.
3. Propose a solution that they might agree to.

Exercise:

Divide your team into pairs. One will be the speaker and one the listener.

Ask the speaker to talk about their journey to work this morning (or something equally mundane).

The listener's role is to actively listen. They need to empathise, paraphrase and ask questions that will continue the focus on the speaker.

Swap roles and repeat.

We know that when the listener assimilates and incorporates what is being said to them it

- Promotes empathy
- Encourages listening and
- Develops the skill of paraphrasing

The outcome should be that the speaker feels that their tale is important and has been taken on board by their listener.

Exercise:

This is a simulation game. You need to set this up ahead of time and write the characters and the scenarios to be pertinent to your business, but not exactly like your business.

Write each character on a separate piece of paper. And then write an agenda for the meeting with a background story to each item.

Set the scene. Your team are either running an imaginary company, charity or city council. Each of your team members are members of the board or council.

Give each member of the team one of the imaginary characters. Assign them against type if you can, so they will have to act accordingly and raise issues according to who they are portraying.

You could assign one of your team to be the chair or you could do it yourself. This depends on how much control you want to have on the outcome.

Then discuss each of the issues and allow the 'players' to have their say in character.

This is a really good exercise for enabling your team members to see different perspectives, allowing them to think things through without relying on team mates, and also engenders a team spirit and collaborative working, and can be a lot of fun.

There is an example at the end of the chapter.

Moral Dilemmas

Lawrence Kohlberg is the father of studies on moral development. He devised a series of moral and ethical questions which he used to promote understanding of moral development. His most well-known 1958 story is as follows:

Heinz's wife is dying from cancer. There is a new drug which might save her. The drug had been discovered by a local chemist, and Heinz tried desperately to buy some for his wife. However, the chemist is charging ten times the money it cost to make the drug, and this is much more than Heinz can afford.

Heinz manages to only raise half the money, even after help from family and friends. He explains to the chemist that his wife is dying and asks if the chemist can let him have it for cheaper, or defer payment.

The chemist refuses, saying that he discovered the drug and is going to make money from it. The husband is desperate to save his wife, so later that night he breaks into the chemist's and steals the drug.

A series of questions was then asked to consider the ethics of the story.

1. Should Heinz have stolen the drug?
2. Would it change anything if Heinz did not love his wife?
3. What if the person dying was a stranger, would it make any difference?
4. Should the police arrest the chemist for murder if the woman died?

These feel a little contrived and there are a lot more pertinent issues that we could be discussing.

1. Should the Covid-19 vaccine be issued to all developing countries for free at the same time as ourselves?

2. What order should be used for distributing Covid-19 vaccinations and why?
3. There are very real decisions that were made by doctors at the start of the pandemic when there were insufficient ventilators. Would you let the patients in their 80s die so that you could give the ventilators to newer patients who are younger?
4. A pair of conjoined twins can be separated resulting in the certain loss of one of them. Should this go ahead?
5. Should drug addicts or smokers be given the same medical care as everyone else?
6. Should you tell your best friend that their spouse is cheating?

Some more global issues that can be discussed:

- Abortion
- Charity
- Animal experimentation
- Capital Punishment
- Euthanasia
- Circumcision (male/female)
- GM Foods
- Editing our unborn kids' genomes
- Animal rights

Example:

Another thought exercise is the "Trolley Dilemma". This is a thought exercise developed by Phillipa Foot in 1967.

There is a runaway trolley (or train) heading for five workers on the line. You don't have sufficient time to alert them. However, you happen to be in a position to pull the lever that will divert the train onto an alternative track. Unfortunately, there is an individual worker on the other line.

- Do you actively divert the train and thus cause the death of the one worker in preference to the five?
- Or do you allow the train to carry on and kill the five?

There is another dimension that can be added to the dilemma. Instead of an alternate track, the train is heading for a bridge. On the bridge is a very large man. Assuming you have the ability, you can throw this man off the bridge, which will stop the train. You will have killed the large man, but saved the five workers on the track.

The ethical issues for the second scenario are more complicated than the first because it involves actively killing someone rather than in the first scenario in which you are deciding who should die.

The point about discussing any of these issues is not to get answers, but to promote discussion. Having your team deliberate about issues that take a lot of thought and consideration is a great tool to help them practise their active listening skills, encourage teamwork, enable individuals to see other points of view.

Tool: Simulation Game

Simulation Game – Town Council

Characters

Below are random characters. You can embellish them if that suits your needs and your proposed agenda, or you can allow the players to embellish them in situ. Often the latter makes for a more interesting event. Feel free to invent your own characters to fit your own agenda and situation.

Cut out each character and pass them to members of your team, making sure that they get to play against type – or even gender. Playing against type is important to engender empathy and complex consideration.

You are Tracy Williams, a young single mother of two children under 10. You have found it difficult to find work since the children were born. You are educated to A Level.

You are Craig Smith, an electrician. You are 26 and single. Recently moved from Manchester, you are finding it hard to make ends meet in London and to find your social niche.

You are Ashma Haque, a young female doctor. You were born in this country but your parents came from Pakistan before you were born. They had an arranged marriage. You live in a multigenerational house with your parents and your grandmother.

You are Joe Peterson, a family man. Sally is your wife. You are a successful businessman and have a wife and two teenage children. You are the sole breadwinner.

You are Sally Peterson, a housewife with two teenage children. Joe is your husband. You are well-educated but gave up work to look after the children.

You are Simon Jones, a widower in his late 60s. Your wife died recently and you are finding it hard to adjust to life without her.

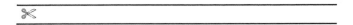

You are Daniel Watts, a gay man in his 40s. You have a high-powered job as a CEO of a large company. You live alone.

You are Melissa Richards, a teacher in your fifties. You are married and your husband is also a teacher. Your children have left home.

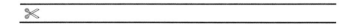

You are Richard Smith, the pastor of the local church. You are married to Linda and have two children in their early teens.

Agenda Issues

1. High cost of funerals. Should funerals be provided by the state?
2. Digital exclusion for low-income families. Should the council be responsible for providing laptops?

3. Arranged marriages of ethnic minority youngsters.
4. Low uptake of Covid-19 vaccine among BAME communities.
5. Prioritise council spending. List the top five areas of expenditure.
6. Providing nursery care for working parents.
7. Gender neutral toilets in public buildings.
8. Charging points for electric cars: Where? Funded by whom?
9. Facilities for dogs
10. Someone on the sex offender's list has just been outed by the public and there are vigilantes regularly outside his house.

Both the characters and the agenda items are entirely random and notional. They might be used as they are if you are just doing an exercise to see how people relate to each other. However, if there are real issues that you would like to see discussed, then feel free to create your own. If you are creating your own issues, it would be helpful to ensure that there are some relevant characters added.

10. Challenge and Change Management

"Fear is a journey, a terrible journey, but sorrow is at least an arrival. When the storm threatens, a man is afraid for his house.
But when the house is destroyed, there is something to do."

Alan Paton in Cry the Beloved Country

Challenge can be scary – or exciting. Both emotions stem from the same physiological response. However, the interpretation of that response is up to you. Both excitement and fear are adrenalin (epinephrine) driven and both produce exactly the same effects in our body – increased heart rate, loss of appetite (sometimes to the extent of nausea), blood diverted to the muscles, increased breathing rate, clammy hands. Therefore, when challenged with something new, some of us are excited and some of us are scared. You will recognise this as the fight/flight syndrome (or sometimes called the fight/fright syndrome). The body needs to ready itself to face danger. You either face the foe and fight, or you flee from the danger. Both require increased flow of adrenalin.

Story:

I have a friend who is in a job that she hates, with little communication between her and her colleagues and very little interaction. She has no enthusiasm for the work and is indifferent to the organisation. She has been there many years and can just amble through the days unengaged and uninterested in what she is doing. She would love to leave, but can't bring herself to do it. She has the experience and skillset to get a really good job but just can't seem to be able to leave.

Every time she gets close, she pulls back at the last minute. She has applied for jobs and even been to two interviews, but never had the gumption to move on.

On one occasion, she was offered a job after going through the selection process, but then pulled out before she had to give her notice "because it didn't feel comfortable".

The reason I relate this story is that my friend was experiencing the 'jitters'. Every time the thought of leaving her old job behind came closer to reality, she stopped the process and returned to the life she was familiar with. It's not that she went away and, after thinking it through, realised that her old job was good after all. No, she just wanted the sense of fear, the jitters, to go away. The best way to alleviate the nerves was simply to return to the routine she was familiar with.

Alan Paton, author of Cry the Beloved Country insightfully said, "Sorrow is better than fear. Fear is a journey, a terrible journey. But sorrow is at least an arriving." How true for my friend. She would rather be in her very unrewarding employment than face the fear of change.

> She was having severe physiological symptoms. However, when she stopped thinking of leaving, the symptoms stopped. Problem solved. Except, of course, that it wasn't.

"Growth and comfort do not coexist. And I think it's a really good thing to remember."

Ginni Rometty

Neuroscientists know that uncertainty makes the brain register as a fault – something that needs to be addressed or repaired. There is dissonance which needs to be corrected. We take the easiest route, the path of least resistance, to correct that discomfort. There is inevitably a sense of loss associated with change.

Change in the workplace can lead to loss of familiarity, loss of competence, loss of comfort, loss of agency – which all lead to loss of self-esteem. It's profound. We feel like we are so out of our depth as to almost feel like we are emotionally drowning. So overwhelmed that we are paralysed.

We tend to talk about the future as looking forward and we look back to the past. The ancients, interestingly, did it the other way around. They would refer to looking forward to the past. We can 'see' what happened, what we did and how things played out. We can visualise where we were, how it felt and what impact our actions had. The future, on the other hand, is completely unknown. We can't 'see' how it plays out or feel how it will feel. It's a complete blank. And this is why they thought of it as looking backward, because they couldn't see it. This is the very essence of what makes it scary. The unknown.

It's not just the physiological response. Along with those feelings come the thoughts. You are having profound feelings and you need to make sense of them. So, you start to rationalise and provide reasons (or, more likely, excuses).

- You are afraid that things won't go to plan. What if I take up that challenge of the new role? I may not be any good at it. I was good in my last role, why rock the boat? If I move on, I won't be able to go back. I don't want to fail.
- It's going to be hard work. Learning new skills, overcoming new issues, becoming familiar with the new environment. It all feels like too much effort.
- You may feel a fear of putting your head above the parapet. Up until now, you have ambled along without gaining too much attention, but now all eyes are on you. People are relying on you and expecting answers from you.
- You may not want to move away from your position in the company as it invites criticism. Remember that middle manager who saw the adversarial nature of the boss versus the staff. The boss is critical of the workers and the workers find the flaws in the managerial style. It's universal. You may fear the criticism that comes with moving away from your comfortable team.
- Fear of the new. You simply don't know how things will turn out and that's scary.

We need to train ourselves to view the future in the way the ancients did. The path ahead is unknown. We don't know if it is straight or windy, hilly or smooth; we don't know if it is bordered by lush foliage or desert sand. We don't even know if it is paved or not. Our job is to construct that path, one step at a time, to recognise that it is our path and we can affect its eventual creation in the ways that we choose. To do this job, we need adrenalin and all the things that go with it. We need the extra muscle power; we need the increased heart rate to bring oxygen to our brains; we need that oxygen to be diverted away from where it is not needed to where it is needed. Start to recognise those jitters as the important physiological response to ready you for the job ahead, rather than an invitation to entertain doubt.

But it's not just nerves; it's also excitement. So why not recognise that we are facing this new path to view new horizons. We can get excited about new responsibilities and being at the helm of new innovations. That is exciting.

Exercise:

Consider a situation which is giving you fear or making you nervous.

Think deeply about what this fear is, what it is composed of, what are the individual issues that make up this fear? Be honest and take your time. It could be in a notebook over several days, or just sketched hurriedly on a post-it note. Whenever you get a glimpse of understanding of what you fear, write it down. The list can be as long or as short as you like, but make sure that it encompasses every consideration. Do this over a protracted period of time. I would suggest at least a week.

Once you have listed your fears, take the time and the effort to address each one individually and attempt to find solutions or explanations.

The things that I fear in taking on this challenge:

1.

2.

3.

4.

5.

6.

So, your list may look something like the table on the following page:

FEARS	EXPLANATION/MITIGATION
a. Unknown	**Unknown**

Clearly, any new situation will present unknowns. Identify what you do know. Recognise all the things that are in your power to change and all those that aren't. Start to visualise the future you are going to put in place once the decision has been made. Ultimately, however, accept that you don't know what it will look like – and that's okay.

| b. Criticism | **Criticism** |

There will always be critics. It's likely to be a bell-shaped curve, where 25% of people love what you are doing, 25% hate it and the rest don't care. Remember that it doesn't matter what criticism you get, as long as you are putting your best effort in. If you do a really good job, there will be less to criticise. Think about all the things you will put in place to mitigate the criticism.

| c. Inadequacy | **Inadequacy** |

You know that you are able to do this next challenge. You have the experience, qualifications and knowledge to take that next step and deliver. Remind yourself of all of your qualities that enable you to carry out this challenge. Remind yourself, too, that it will be a learning curve in the beginning, and put a plan in place to ensure that learning and development will take place.

d. Loneliness	**Loneliness**
	They do say that it's lonely at the top, but not if you bring people with you. Make sure that your team are working with you to effect this new change. Continue to challenge them, too, as individuals and see how they grow in stature and competence.
e. Resistance	**Resistance**
	Resistance is only ever short-lived. People learn how to live with the new changes and systems very quickly. They, like you, are just unfamiliar, and that lack of familiarity engenders fear. You will be able to justify the changes and bring comfort to those who are resisting.

This is a made-up list, but the issues are likely to be very real to many people. And this would be my take on addressing them.

In order to minimise resistance from your staff, there are ways you can include them in the development of the change and ways that you can encourage buy-in.

Tool: Some exercises for helping your staff to feel comfortable about the change.

1. Most people are on Facebook nowadays (or any number of other social media platforms). Ask your staff team to think about the last time the platform changed its layout or look. Invite them to articulate how that felt, to remember the

---

amount of complaining they or people on their contacts list did. This new change will be just like that. They can now hardly remember what it was they liked or why they were so resistant.

2. At the next team meeting, ask everyone to choose one person to observe (or allocate them). They must note their behaviour during the meeting and note all the things that they observe to be different to themselves. This is an excellent way to encourage your team members to consider that difference and diversity is normal. Other ways of doing things work just as well. Without provoking or insulting, bring the observations to plenum for discussion.

3. Collect a number of objects from around the office – the more obscure the better. Show the team the first object and then pass it around. Don't name it or say what it is or where it comes from. Allow everyone to get a good idea of how it looks and feels. Now challenge them to invent a new use for it. Everyone gets a turn to describe their new use for the item. This demonstrates the huge array of perspectives. It's a fun exercise, but gives insight to other ways of thinking about exactly the same object.

4. Have two white boards or flip chart pages. One labelled 'positive' and the other, 'negative'. Brain-storm all the words you can come up with about change – e.g. transform, modify, alter, vary etc. Give everyone a wad of sticky notes. They write each of their words on a separate note. Then they place their note on the

appropriate board – either positive or negative. Once all notes have been placed, discuss each word in turn and show that all words can be thought of as either. Thinking of these words in a positive way will actually help to move forward.

5. You could construct a simulation game, asking your team to develop and sell a product. About 10 minutes in, after they have assigned roles and begun the planning process, add another dimension. Do this again ten minutes later … several times. After the exercise is completed, lead a discussion about the frustrations of having new parameters. Explore their feelings and their actions.

11. Stretch, Encourage and Challenge

"The mind is not a vessel that needs filling, but wood that needs igniting."

Plutarch

Skill Development

Encouraging your team members to develop new skills will have a positive effect in a variety of ways. Remember Sophie with the new job, and the line manager in another city? Had she started the job by undergoing training in a specific area of the job, she could then have gone on to concentrate on that area, hone her new skills, and be very confident that what she was doing was in line with the requirements of the job. Without any training whatsoever, other than a perfunctory induction, she was lost.

The main reasons for training your workforce are:

- Inculcates appropriate knowledge acquisition
- Keeps them interested and engaged in their work
- Creates a professional team
- Encourages personal development
- Makes the workforce feel valued

- Addresses weaknesses
- Improves performance which will translate to greater productivity

Training can be specifically tailored or you could access proprietary external training. If you are in a small organisation, arranging and carrying out in-house training might be difficult if you don't have someone with the correct skill-set. However, where possible, it is often best. Designing your own training will be tailor made for the organisation's needs and for the needs of the individuals undergoing the training. However, it is only best when there is an appropriate person to deliver the training.

Story:

Martha was in a middle management position in a charity with 60 employees nationally. She often used to get very frustrated with the poor evaluation after events, and the resultant failure to learn from experience. Through the correct channels, she made it clear that she thought that the management team should be offered a training session on evaluation at a forthcoming monthly meeting.

She received a communique from central management that they agreed that it was necessary and would ensure it would happen. They were looking into the logistics of setting it up.

Two weeks later, she received a telephone call from a colleague, another middle manager, asking her to run training for the management team on evaluation. It wasn't clear if he knew about her complaints or not, but it seemed entirely inappropriate for him to be inviting her to deliver the training. Clearly, she knows something about evaluation from previous employment (which is why she recognised that it was poor), but she wasn't qualified to teach it.

Commercial training is slick and employs experienced trainers. Their courses are tried and tested, and improved over many deliveries. However, sometimes they use misleading advertising to procure the clients. The following story illustrates how a commercial company obtains clients through misleading and ambiguous claims. They employ poor facilitators and manage the material centrally, so that facilitators have no ownerships or knowledge. This is not to knock commercial concerns. Most are highly professional and excellent at what they do, but it does illustrate that you have to be careful in procuring the appropriate training outfit. Research thoroughly and follow reviews and recommendations.

Story:

A supply teacher, Bernard, attended a two-day training session to ensure that he is up-to-date with his teaching. As a supply teacher he doesn't have access to the CPD offered in schools, so was always keen to update his skills and knowledge when the opportunity arose.

He was invited by e-mail from his agency recommending a course referred to as (and I paraphrase here) "Classroom Team", with a subtext about positive handling techniques. As a supply teacher Bernard often finds himself in a room with ancillary staff. He thought that this would be an ideal opportunity to brush up on his ability to best include these colleagues and to utilise their skills most effectively and efficiently. The word "Team" in the title encouraged him that it would be a very useful course.

He soon learned that the course was in fact about physically restraining pupils. He had not realised, when signing up for the course that "handling" was a literal term. He had been teaching for many years and had yet to encounter a situation where he had to physically restrain a pupil. I am not saying that it doesn't happen, but it is not the top skill that one considers acquiring. I know that *in extremis*, I would call for a colleague to restrain a pupil, but I have never needed to, and neither had Bernard.

You would like to think that an individual tasked with teaching a bunch of teachers, might want to hone their skills and demonstrate their best facilitation abilities. Not

---

so. Bernard witnessed some of the worst presentation/facilitation he had seen in a long time. The presenters were amiable enough and engaging enough, but he could not recommend them as teachers.

The following is just a handful of poor presentation skills they displayed:

1. The course material is written centrally and disseminated for presenters to deliver. It was obvious that they had not prepared by reading through the slides first.
   a. There were numerous mistakes, to the point that several sentences or points were entirely unintelligible
   b. Video clips were not added to the presentation as links, meaning that presenters had to stop the presentation each time and then look for a video clip in the files – time-consuming, unprofessional and lacking in preparation
   c. Presenters simply read through each of the slides without offering depth or understanding. In fact, there was very little enthusiasm or even expression in their voices. They were just going through the motions.
2. At one point the next slide said "Tea Break!!!" (Why all the exclamation marks?). It was a full 25 minutes before they broke for tea, because the painful end to each session was a round robin of each participant in turn sharing what they had learned.

3. When opening up the floor for feedback or "take out" messages (Bernard asked for a sweet and sour chicken, but the humour was lost on them), facilitators repeatedly allowed for lengthy "confessionals" (participants who feel the need to lengthily share an episode in their life that is only remotely connected with the subject under discussion).

4. At one point participants were asked for ideas about their rights and responsibilities in the classroom. Bernard offered that one right (and equally a responsibility) is maintenance of a conducive learning environment. The facilitator wrote down "safe environment", and then scrubbed that and wrote "comfortable". It is always best to write down exactly what the contributor has said – even if they are wrong. You can discuss corrections and amendments later. She later admitted that she had no idea what the word "conducive" means.

5. Course materials were inexact. A quiz that participants were asked to complete at the start used ambiguous language. For instance, they had watched about 10 minutes' worth of slides extolling the virtues of self-restraint. A question then came up in the quiz about how important restraint is. Turns out that the intention, in this context, was physical restraint of the pupils.

6. Every time a challenging question was put to the facilitators, they would remind participants that this is just a "basic" course. If they want serious skills in this field, they must sign up for the

advanced course. They had no background knowledge whatsoever. Neither of them was a trained teacher, and couldn't answer most of the participants' questions.

7. At one point, a visiting colleague, from the company, who was in the room observing the facilitators, sought to vindicate the poor performance. She made a huge song and dance about the fact that this is only the second time the pair had delivered this particular course. I would say that this was all the more reason they should have reviewed their material, corrected mistakes and performed a run-through to ensure that they understood what they were delivering. Lack of familiarity with the course materials is not a valid excuse for not doing the groundwork. Indeed, it is the reason to do the groundwork. Bernard had paid good money to attend, and he expects the same good quality that someone attending their hundredth delivery gets.

In summary, the speakers had not prepared themselves adequately by familiarising themselves with the material; had not done sufficient background reading and research; had not familiarised themselves with the clientele and their prior knowledge, background and reasons for wanting to join the course; had not familiarised themselves with the inspiration and background behind each slide and each activity.

In short, if you are going to teach a teacher, make sure that your teaching skills are up to scratch. Indeed, if you

> are going to do any teaching, make sure that you are familiar with what you are teaching.

This story just serves to illustrate the need to choose a suitable training company if you are going down that route.

This company was unscrupulous. They access clients via teaching agencies, and their materials and delivery are subpar. Most training companies are very professional and employ capable trainers.

Happier and more productive staff

People love to be in a position of knowledge and competence. The thought of taking them out of their comfort zone by expecting them to acquire a new skill can be scary. However, the flipside of this is that without new skills or unfamiliar tasks, they will become bored and unstimulated.

Stimulation

Stimulation achieves the following:

- **Improves learning**

When we are mentally stimulated, we are engrossed in our work and more alert. This makes taking on new tasks and skills a much more fruitful exercise. Remember how you were in history at school? (It was history for me, but for you may have been another subject). I was completely unengaged, wasn't able to analyse or take on board any dates or facts, struggled to remember information for the exams.

- **Improves focus**

A stimulated brain is an interested mind. When we are stimulated, it heightens our interest and we become engrossed in the new information or gain an area of expertise.

- **Self-actualisation**

This is a term in psychology to reflect a person who has reached their full potential in every sphere of their lives. Many counsellors strive to achieve this in their clients. Personally, to me it feels like chasing rainbows. Yes, it would be desirable to have achieved our potential, but I don't believe that we can ever be exposed to everything that can elicit our full potential. I don't believe that there is ever any way of even knowing what our full potential is. I found a list of qualities of a self-actualised person. Included on the list was "They Tend to be Problem Centred", as if this was a good thing. Being Problem centred is never a good thing. We need to be **Solution** Focused (see chapter 13).

I believe that a much more helpful device is "Human Givens". The Human Givens is predicated on a set of needs which we always need to fulfil. You might have heard of Maslow's Hierarchy of Needs. The list of Needs is: Physiological, Safety, Love and Belonging, and Esteem, with each one needing to be fulfilled before we can go on to the next, culminating in Self Actualisation.

The Human Givens concentrates only on our emotional needs. And the list does not need to be fulfilled in any particular order.

- **Security** – safe territory and an environment which allows us to develop fully

- **Attention** (to give and receive it) – a form of nutrition
- **Sense of autonomy and control** – having volition to make responsible choices
- **Emotional intimacy** – to know that at least one other person accepts us totally for who we are, "warts 'n' all"
- **Feeling part of a wider community**
- **Privacy** – opportunity to reflect and consolidate experience
- **Sense of status** within social groupings – knowing that you have a place
- **Sense of competence and achievement**
- **Meaning and purpose** – which come from being stretched in what we do and think.

Being able to take responsibility of your own mental well-being in this way is important to gain control of your thoughts, feelings and behaviour. You could construct this spreadsheet template and send it to each member of the team to fill out in order to monitor their own well-being. Obviously, this would be a private exercise for each person, but you could raise it with individuals at your next appraisal meeting, asking if there is anything that they would like the organisation to address to raise their scores.

Date	Security — safe territory and an environment which allows us to develop fully		Attention (to give and receive it) — a form of nutrition		Sense of autonomy and control — having volition to make responsible choices		Emotional intimacy — to know that at least one other person accepts us totally for who we are, "warts 'n' all"		Feeling part of a wider community		Privacy — opportunity to reflect and consolidate experience		Sense of status within social groupings		Sense of competence and achievement		Meaning and purpose — which come from being stretched in what we do and think.		Average
My score/Out of:	My score	10	My score	10	My score	10	My score	10	My score	10	My score	10	My score	10	My score	10	My score	10	
	0%		0%		0%		0%		0%		0%		0%		0%		0%		0.00%
	0%		0%		0%		0%		0%		0%		0%		0%		0%		0.00%
	0%		0%		0%		0%		0%		0%		0%		0%		0%		0.00%
	0%		0%		0%		0%		0%		0%		0%		0%		0%		0.00%
	0%		0%		0%		0%		0%		0%		0%		0%		0%		0.00%
	0%		0%		0%		0%		0%		0%		0%		0%		0%		0.00%
	0%		0%		0%		0%		0%		0%		0%		0%		0%		0.00%
	0%		0%		0%		0%		0%		0%		0%		0%		0%		0.00%

Thinking

Many organisations expect their staff to blindly follow the instructions that they have been given. Places of work that have this philosophy engender unhappy staff. Without agency, we are mere automatons doing our master's bidding.

1. All too often a set of rules or directives causes laziness. We'll do exactly what we have been asked to do and no more.
2. It can cause frustration when an employee knows a much better way to do things but is feeling constrained by the framework of rules and guidelines.
3. It can restrict creativity and innovation. If an employee knows that their ideas are outside of the guidelines, they won't bother to present them or to even try to come up with new ideas.

Create an environment of having your staff think for themselves – and for the company. Not only will they feel invested in the company and continue to do their utmost to ensure its continued success, but they will feel content and fulfilled.

Retention

Remember the story at the beginning, the new CEO who gave pens as an alleged incentive? I left the organisation soon after and I later found out that the CEO herself left three months after I did. That competitive edge thing is not good for the spirit; it makes people unhappy, unfulfilled and frustrated.

We need to keep our staff happy if we want to avoid a high turnover. Happiness is achieved by all the things we instinctively know: good remuneration, pleasant environment, perks, affable and collaborative team, flexible working conditions … and many more. I would highlight that at the top of that list should be acknowledgement. Nobody wants to work without recognition.

Co-Leaders for Every Project

By placing two people in charge of a project (or at least one lead and one deputy), you remove any risk of overwhelming a single person. You also have someone to deputise if necessary. You never know when people are going to be off for personal reasons, health emergencies or they may just decide to resign. Having someone else to take over the reins in these instances is invaluable.

Knowledge is shared and augmented. You have ideas from two people. Often, when one person working alone is trying to come up with new ideas, they are just cycling the same thoughts and find it very difficult to move forward. With the addition of another person to bounce ideas off, not only are you getting two sources of new ideas but they will often spark against each other, in a synergistic way, to create a much better third idea, or develop the original idea to a much more honed one.

Strength

If one person is working solo on a project, it lacks credibility. The minute you have two people leading a team, it gains strength and validity. Each leader in the partnership has influence in different spheres and is able to call upon different people from their personal contacts – to either validate the project or offer assistance or resources. Pooling expertise and experience also has a huge benefit to the strength of the project. A two-person leadership team for every project means having to set aside personal interests and strive towards the common goal.

That strength is also important when one person has to be off work due to sickness, or on holiday. Normally, the work of a team would just stagnate while the leader was away (unless there were constant electronic directives from the team leader). However, with a second leader, everything can just continue under his or her guidance.

Having two people to lead each team avoids the lengthy handover process if someone leaves the organisation. It costs staff time, is boring for both the person who is leaving and the person taking over, who is likely to only retain a small percentage of what they have been told.

Everybody is knowledgeable. Remember the Zone of Proximal Development in chapter 4? We work best when we are learning from each other – and teaching each other – seeing others' perspectives, gaining skills that our colleagues can teach us. Having a two-person leadership team means that they are constantly learning from each other.

Precious Knowledge

Story:

Craig was responsible for partner development, based in the head office in London. He had been in the job for several years and had made it his own. Craig was old school. He was proud of his hard back A4 journal which he carried with him everywhere and would write notes which he then referred to when a similar circumstance arose. Whenever he went to a new partner, whatever arose, he could refer back to his notes and see what he did in similar circumstances; or he could refer back to the last time he visited someone and see what he did or said. Except, of course, that he couldn't. Leafing endlessly through his handwritten notes, he wasn't always able to find the notes he was looking for as they were in chronological order which he wasn't able to search systematically, and he didn't keep an electronic diary which he could search. Indeed, sometimes the notes for a particular partner were in an older journal. His one great skill was that he had a fantastic memory and often didn't need to refer to notes. This, of course, made him invaluable to the organisation as the repository of all the important information.

There was no system of checks and balances, no evaluation of what worked well and what didn't, no account of the variables, nor any collaboration with colleagues. In short, there was no means of reproducing his effort for different partners. If someone wanted to know about a particular partner, they would have to ask Craig.

After he had been with the company for 9 years, he was joined by Barry who was based in the regions. Barry became the Regional Partners Director working under Craig as the

Partners Director. The idea was that Barry would eventually take over from Craig when he retired.

Craig was excited. At 48, he had never been a line manager and was looking forward to telling Barry how to do the job. Barry, however, was not the sensitive, responsive sort of worker that Craig was, and wasn't able to retain all the information that was in Craig's head. Craig had stories about all the families, knew everyone's back stories, hiccups and hurdles, as well as all the personal good news stories such as weddings and children. All completely extraneous information, but it helped him understand his work. Barry was of a scientific bent; he needed facts and figures, evidence and reproducible systems. At Barry's induction, Craig advised Barry to buy a large hard bound journal to write all of his notes. Of course, Barry balked at this notion.

After a while in the job, left to his own devices, Barry started to put all of his information onto spreadsheets and databases; he devised a novel reporting template so that he could record all the important information in one place for any of their colleagues to see, at a glance, all the necessary facts and figures about each partner – including a place for Craig's more visceral take. This was then easily transferable to a spreadsheet for ease of comparison. He also developed several strategies for gleaning the facts and figures that he needed, when he went into the different branches. He organised his computer files so that it was very easy for anyone to navigate in the shared drive.

Before long, the Executive Director called Barry into his office and directed him to teach Craig how to do the work that he was doing. Barry was being asked to manage his manager.

Ironically, shortly after, in a directors' meeting, the HR manager was doing an exercise with the directors' team. She asked each person to say one thing that they would like to be their legacy if they were to leave the organisation tomorrow. Craig's answer was that he would like to have someone in place that he could pass on his work to.

This story is quite sad because Craig still thought that he had something to hand over, thought that his modus operandi was valuable. His expectations were never met when Barry came on board, and were unlikely to ever be met. He thought he was line managing, but was asked to follow his reportee; he thought that he held the golden chalice to how the work should be done, but someone came along and developed something far superior and reproducible; he thought that his systems were exemplary and wanted to hand them over to his successor, but his systems were mere dust compared to the robust enduring ones that Barry had put in place.

The saddest part of all was that, despite being told to work with the systems that Barry had developed, despite the ED telling him that he needs to scrap his journals in favour of Barry's reporting templates, and despite the organisation having adopted all of Barry's innovations, Craig still felt that he wanted someone to inherit his antiquated method of working.

If anything, it is an indictment on the HR team who consulted with Craig before Barry was appointed. They should have:

1. given him management training
2. discussed his legacy and what was worth handing to Barry and what needed to be discarded or revised
3. managed his performance on an ongoing basis
4. importantly, they should have helped him to evaluate his work

They say that knowledge is power. It definitely feels like that in an organisation where people are competing for power and guarding their knowledge. Those with knowledge of how things are done, or background knowledge about the people or projects, will often keep it to themselves. Being the only one with that information is perceived to put them at an advantage in the organisation. Unfortunately, it actually puts the **organisation** at a disadvantage.

Sharing knowledge can potentially lead to creation of a much larger pool of knowledge. Craig in the story above was not keen to share his knowledge. He felt that it was the only thing that kept him where he was. Barry improved the organisation by finding succinct ways to share.

Once knowledge is shared, it is not only held by additional people but is enhanced by having those people interact with it and add to it.

Barry's template for knowledge sharing gave everyone in the organisation access to all knowledge and gave them a way of sharing their own knowledge and adding it to the pool. In fact, while Barry was still developing his template and had saved his draft versions for one or two partners he had worked with, he had people from within the organisation phoning him to update him on things that they knew about that partner.

Purely by making it possible to share, Barry had enhanced organisational sharing.

Everyone Is Knowledgeable

Staff should be collaborating both within teams and across teams. It invites new perspectives and encourages innovation.

Tool:

An excellent way to encourage collaboration is the following exercise which encourages both sharing of ideas, and analysis and evaluation of what the organisation is doing.

Stage 1.

1. Brainstorm the key elements of what your organisation does. Whether it is sales or services, you will probably create a list from everyone's contributions.

Stage 2.

2. Take the three most salient items on the list and put each as a heading on a sheet of flip chart paper. A fourth flip chart sheet has "Other" as its heading.

3. Place them around the room, one on each wall if possible.

4. Give each participant a wad of Post-it notes.

5. While still seated, participants write something on a sticky note, such as a response or comment, about each of the headings. If they have several separate thoughts about a heading, they should write a separate sticky note for each.

6. Participants place their notes on the relevant posters and then return to their seats.

Stage 3.

7. When all participants are seated, invite them to now spend some time perusing all the comments and "dialoguing" with them. They should be given plenty of time for this stage. Allow them to peruse all the posters and wander round the room as if it is a gallery; read all the other Post-it notes and write their own in response, wherever they feel they have a response – placing it below the comment they are responding to. This might become multi-layered if people then choose to respond to responses. Allow this to happen. When all have completed this stage, they should return to their seats.

Stage 4.

8. Divide the participants into four groups. Each group gets one of the flip chart pages.
9. With their own sheet, each group puts the Post-it notes into order, discarding duplicate ideas, grouping together like comments and developing a theme or sequence if they can.
10. Once they have all analysed their own poster, the next task is to present it to the others.

This works best if the facilitator then takes it all away and tabulates the results to be presented at a later meeting. The table should have two columns. (Alternatively, a second team meeting can address the analysis phase).

The first is just the raw data of the Post-it notes. The second is ideas – either from the Post-it note dialogues or from the facilitator after the event.

What we think or believe. Or What is the status quo? Or Themes that arose	How can we address this? Solutions

The beauty of this exercise is that the facilitator then e-mails the findings and ideas back to the participants, and a continued dialogue should be encouraged, allowing the team to have their say about what the facilitator has concluded. Also, having finished the exercise, they may have come away with additional thoughts. Encourage them to share these.

12. Value All Viewpoints

"You never really understand a person until you consider things from his point of view... until you climb into his skin and walk around in it."

Harper Lee, 1960, in "To Kill a Mockingbird"

Without seeing other viewpoints, we are blinkered, only seeing things from one perspective and failing to take account of our stakeholders, customers or colleagues. Our businesses and organisations rely on the goodwill of those with whom we work. We should find ways of understanding their needs, and offering them what they want from us.

Team Building Exercises

Team building exercises are good for teasing out communication between colleagues and promoting understanding between teammates and across departments.

We are all familiar with the team building exercises such as building the highest tower out of some spaghetti and marshmallows, or creating an egg protection device that will allow you to throw an egg from a height without it breaking. There are many more such activities and, despite having become a bit hackneyed, they do serve a purpose.

We talk about team building but we don't stop to recognise what that means. Yes, they are fun ways to engender communication and enhance mutual understanding. But, why?

The point about team building exercises is that they are an opportunity to hear other viewpoints and trial them in a no risk environment. By listening to other members of the team and allowing them to trial their ideas, we are learning to trust that person, and give credence to their ideas. This trust can later be translated to the real-world issues that we face in the workplace.

Tool:

Below is a brief list of some ideas to engender team building and trust in other viewpoints.

1. Graffiti wall

In a shared space or thoroughfare, construct a graffiti wall by placing lining paper over a large surface. In the centre, in bold letters (or on a laminated sheet stuck to the "wall") place an issue that the company has been deliberating. Place some marker pens (on strings, so they don't "walk") for people to add their comments as and when they feel like it. Give it a deadline (no longer than a month), and tell staff when it will be coming down.

This is a great way for people to express their sentiments anonymously without fear of judgement or embarrassment. It is also a great way for management to find out what the staff really think. Some comments might promote "water cooler discussions" or just set a series of graffiti comments and responses in motion.

---

2. Consensus tool

Write "Meaningful" and "Pleasant" as headings on a white board. Ask everyone to comment what would make the organisation's work either meaningful or pleasant, or what you already do that is either of these. You could use Post-it notes for this. If you are not using Post-it notes, get each person to call out their ideas in turn and construct a mind map. Otherwise, stick the notes to the board to create links. Once all the responses are in, and the mind map has been constructed, try to reach a consensus about each contribution, starting with the contributor defending their idea and explaining it. Listening to all the viewpoints creates common ground and promotes common values.

3. Story telling

Each person takes it in turn to tell a story about their work experiences, using a theme. Like the music exercise in chapter 2, this helps people to get to know each other in a relaxed way and encourages the team to listen to each other. Sometimes a work-based experience can be illuminating for management to see changes that need to be made.

4. Opinion Spectrum

Get the team to offer suggestions on a topic. This could be something contentious within the organisation, or something more global. Get them to each write their perspective on a sticky note. In discussion, then map out the different perspectives, as a progressive list or as a mind map. This exercise recognises the variety of views and illustrates how each view has its place in the entire scheme.

5. Back of an envelope

In small teams of no more than 4, give the group a problem – either real world or imaginary. Give them an envelope and fifteen minutes to create a flow chart of what needs to be done to address this problem on the back of the envelope. At the end of fifteen minutes the teams present their ideas and decide, as a group, which was best. You may wish to extend the exercise by getting the group to deliberate and decide how to incorporate all the ideas into one integrated flow chart. Promotes discussion and encourages listening to all viewpoints. The reason the envelope is used is to encourage paring to the bare minimum and distilling the information into a clear plan.

6. Tabloid versus broadsheet

Divide the group into two teams. Each team is assigned either tabloid or broadsheet. Considering the same project that your organisation is working on (or the organisation itself), each team has to produce a front page in their particular newspaper style. They have to consider what gets featured, how it is presented, headlines, featured articles, pictures (these can be mocked up). This is a great exercise for agreeing on division of labour, possibly creating content against their own beliefs, and it encourages them to visualise. Discussion is engendered when agreeing on what is included, and how the information is turned into newsworthy print material. With larger numbers, the exercise could be expanded to have several different newspapers representing different views on the political spectrum.

> ### 7. Dragons' Den (Shark Tank in the US)
> Teams come up with novel ideas for their projects, and pitch them to the management. The pitch has to include, brand name, slogan, marketing strategy and business plan. Possibly, could also include a financial plan. These don't have to be real or executable ideas. The exercise promotes creative thinking and collaboration and encourages development of seeing the perspective of the work they do from the eyes of a stakeholder or investor.

Environment Matters

I worked for a Not-for-Profit organisation once. The environment was very typical of most archetypal office environments. We each sat in little cubicles; the windows didn't open and we relied on air conditioning; no private spaces and all neighbouring cubicle phone-calls were overheard. It was noisy and the artificial lighting was grim. It was a very depressing environment. Office hours were rigidly 9 to 5.

Contrast this with the environments that the big tech companies have created. Wide open spaces, bright colourful environments with access to outside spaces, movable furniture, loosely defined desk spaces, many opportunities and spaces for interacting with colleagues, no definitive office hours.

I know someone who works for one of these companies. He lives in New York but never seems to be in the country. He is allowed as much time off as he likes, doesn't have to report his hours to anyone. As long as he is doing his work and getting the results, he can do pretty much whatever he likes. Compared to his previous job, where he was stuck in a small office, he admits that his productivity is way higher under these conditions.

The company provides a bunch of other perks, such as life insurance, parental leave, paid time off, discounts, health insurance, and many more. Their website adds that they provide "fitness classes, gym memberships, massage, personal trainers, childcare, eldercare, pet care, house cleaning, tax preparation, and student loan repayments". However, it is the work-life balance that takes primacy in making this a fabulous company to work for.

We can't all provide all of these benefits, particularly if we are running a small organisation, but all organisations and companies would do well to learn about the psychology of this attitude against the classic methodology of working in silos. Happy staff are much more effective, and they will make the company much more effective.

There are things that we can put in place on a smaller scale that would greatly enhance staff socialising and better workplace environments. For instance, placing a table tennis table (or a selection of board games) where people can spend their break times, giving them enough break time to recharge, regardless of how long that takes, valuing them for their output rather than the hours that they put in.

The old view that we have to sit at our desks from 9 to 12:30 and then again from 1:30 to 5 − to clock in and account for our time − is outdated, counterproductive, and should be reviewed.

Concentrating on Leadership Is Folly

Leaders usually meet regularly to discuss the running of the organisation, make decisions for their workforce and decide the direction of the company. This can be a very restricting way to run the company. Let's not forget that it is the workforce who are on the ground and know what is happening. They are engaging face to face with our partners, stakeholders and customers. They are the ones who know how things are actually operating and what is really going on in the workings of the organisation.

I once worked for a NFP organisation where my colleagues were constantly referring to how we can be improving what we offer to our stakeholder leaders. I often had to remind them that the service we are offering is not just for the leadership, but for the general membership. For one thing, these are the people who will be benefiting from our implementations. But, also, if we continue to think along the lines that my colleagues were thinking, these are the people who will potentially become the leaders of tomorrow. If they recognise a snub now, they may not be amenable to working with us when they become leaders.

Evolution of Agreement

If you were to canvass your workforce on their favourite musician by e-mail or written form, the chances are that you would get a vast array and very little overlap. However, if you were to conduct that same assessment in a discussion, you might find a lot more agreement. In discussion, people are reminded of the merits of singers they had forgotten about and may be persuaded by some of the qualities of a particular band.

This is akin to workplace opinions on the work you are doing. If people are not being persuaded by other viewpoints, development of the work is inhibited; progress is dependent on cycling one's own thoughts without any fresh input. Having meetings with colleagues, sharing the leadership of projects, and listening to an array of viewpoints enhances the evolution of that project.

Culture makes a difference, too. People from different cultures see the world in a different way, and we can learn from others who have had life experiences that we have not. I, for instance, am a TCK, a Third Culture Kid. This is someone who grew up somewhere (or many places) other than their passport culture. They find that they no longer fit in to their passport culture, but neither do they fit in to their host culture. They create a "third culture" where they have more in common with other people with similar experiences than they do with people either from their passport or their host culture. TCKs bring a new viewpoint to many situations.

Being a TCK comes with a variety of perspectives and specific cultural nuances. Living in a monoculture makes it difficult to be aware of other ways of seeing things, other ways of behaving and interacting. Everybody has the ability to adopt the attributes that a TCK is naturally imbued with – observation, tolerance, open-mindedness, adaptivity, better at communication, and even often multilingual. We just have to consciously learn these skills, and first recognise that they are desirable skills. I call them skills rather than attributes because they can be gained.

Story:
The following is an illustration of how language alters our perception.

I have a friend, Kevin, who was living in a Mediterranean country known for their brash mannerisms, and he spoke the language fluently, although he was a native English speaker. Locals are known for being outspoken, loud and animated – which can be seen as aggressive to outside observers. They can often be overly familiar.

I once observed Kevin on the phone to one of his Mediterranean colleagues. He was standing up, used his hands very animatedly, and both his language and tone were loud and assertive.

When that call finished, I observed him on a phone call with a fellow English speaker in the same company. His entire manner changed. He sat down and seemed more demure. There were no hand gestures, and his tone was calm and deliberate, almost deferential.

Same person, same job, same situation, 10 minutes apart. Only difference was the language he was speaking.

This just serves to illustrate that language acquisition changes us as people, not just the words we use, but our entire demeanour.

We can all acquire a new language or learn the mores of another society, much as we can learn to be tolerant, open-minded and adaptive. All of these attributes help us to see other viewpoints.

13. Solutions Focus

"The solution often turns out more beautiful than the puzzle."

Richard Dawkins

Have you ever noticed that, even when scientists are certain about something, it is still called a theory, never a fact? The theory of relativity, the theory of evolution, cell theory, ... and so on. A theory is something that is widely accepted, and for which there is a great deal of evidence.

So why do we not call them scientific facts. The reason is that scientists are not so arrogant as to believe that they have the answers. They recognise that new "facts" may emerge or be generated over time. The way science works is that ideas are translated into experiments, experiments are conducted and data obtained. Data is not evidence. Just because something happened, it doesn't mean that it always happens. From the raw data, interpretations are made and theories postulated. Once they have been determined to be robust – reproducible and accurate – experiment design and the resulting data and interpretations are published. Once in the scientific public domain, other scientists try to pull it apart or reproduce it and affirm it as a confirmed theory. This analysis and constructive criticism continue until it is either disproved or updated. Until then it is accepted theory.

Hence it will always be a theory – awaiting proof, but with sufficient evidence to hold it as true. Scientists don't hold on to the questions that they had, or the original problem that sent them looking for an explanation. They focus on finding the solution. Remember, they start with an idea, and then design an experiment around that idea.

It seems obvious. If we want to effect change, we need to concentrate on solutions, but we don't. We tend to focus on problems.

When we construct a jigsaw puzzle, we don't look at all the pieces in the box and reflect on what a miserable situation we have. No, we look at the front of the box and recognise what we are trying to achieve. We then set about looking at the solution – first the edge bits, then the colour patterns.

One step at a time, slowly, we solve our problem **because we know what the solution looks like**. This is what we need to do in the work environment, too – or indeed, any environment.

We spend hours in meetings examining the problem, trying to understand the problem. We give it a name and an identity. We try to work out how the problem arose, describe the problem, establish who is to blame for the problem, analyse the development of the problem … and so on. And when you are problem-focused you become frustrated and despondent. The result is that it starts to take over our efforts, and nothing positive gets done. All you have done is created a biography of a problem.

Is this approach getting you anywhere? Has it helped you to **solve** the problem or to move any closer to changing the way things are done? I've heard it described by one Solutions Focus practitioner as going to the supermarket with a shopping list of things you don't want, leaving you to extrapolate, from that very long list, the things that you do want.

If only we spent that time on solutions, we would be much more effective and efficient. The thing is that if we are focusing on the problem, we will never see the solution that is often right in front of us. It's like only focusing on one plane of vision under the microscope. Yet all of the samples are three dimensional, they have depth. If we played around with the focus knobs a little, we would find a plane that offers what we are looking for. We all have that one thing (or things) that is working well. We just don't concentrate on it. We concentrate on the things that are going badly or that we are no good at. We want to improve; we want to know why we are so bad at it.

Origins of Solutions Focus

Solutions Focus arose out of the world of psychotherapy, where it was at first called Quick Therapy. Counsellors and coaches working with clients could get them to move forward in their lives by getting them to envisage what it was that they wanted in life. The remarkable benefits in mental health were soon translated from the personal to the professional. Organisations and companies, educational institutes, and many other spheres, have all been introduced to Solutions Focussed thinking, with very little adaptation and tremendous success in change management.

The psychologist, might have a client who is depressed, for whom "everything" is going wrong and they come for help. The psychologist will probe to find out what is actually going **well** and ignore everything that is going wrong. They will ask the client for a figure out of ten of how they are feeling compared to how they would like to be feeling. Whatever the figure the client comes back with – even if it's 1 out of 10 – this represents 10% going well. The simple answer is do more of that. The psychologist will now probe about all that is going well and help the client to do more in that vein.

So how does that work for the world of work? I am a high school teacher. In the class room, I will often get complaints from the pupils about something that was said or done by another. They want retribution; they want the other kid to be punished, or at least rebuked. If I punish or rebuke the kid, I am not solving anything. He may still do it again. What we really want is for the perpetrator to stop. Instead, I will first remind them that whatever they are complaining about is in the past. We can't go back and make it not have happened. (In other words, we stop focusing on the problem). What we can do is find ways for it not to continue happening (focus on the solution). I then ask them what they would like me to do about it. There are many options that are often used in the classroom. The teacher can ask the pupil being hit to:

1. Walk away and let it go
2. Tell the perpetrator to stop
3. Move the recipient to another seat
4. Discuss how they are feeling in light of being hit
5. Seek an apology

6. Talk it out with each other
7. Ignore it and get on with their work
8. Go somewhere else for a few minutes to cool off

A quick look at this list will show that some of these options are not actually going to solve the problem. Clearly, they don't want it to happen again. I will, in discussion, get them to recognise that a rebuke from the teacher won't go any way to making them feel better about what happened. Together, they need to reach a solution which is either for the other kid to agree to desist, or to move him to another seat.

I recognise that this is a facile example, but it illustrates that we can only move forward, and it illustrates the three facets of Solutions Focused thinking.

1. Describe what we want to achieve (the other pupil to stop calling him names or hitting him)
2. Identify what is working well (when I am looking at them, or when they are seated away from each other, the behaviour stops)
3. Take small steps (ask him first to desist, and then move him if he doesn't)

Story:

A wonderful example of Solutions Focus being employed, before it was even conceived, is the archetypally British solution created by Harold Macmillan's Ministry of Defence civil servants.

Harold MacMillan was the Prime Minister during the height of the cold war. It was inconceivable that he would be out of contact in the event of a nuclear emergency, perhaps requiring retaliation. As Prime Minister, Macmillan often had to be on the road, and out of communication with his cabinet. Of course, this was long before the days of the mobile phone.

Civil servants had to find a way for MacMillan to be able to make a phone call while he was on the road.

They looked at what was already in existence and working well. In those days, the Automobile Association (AA), as well as having an extensive fleet of vans on the road, had a national network of phones on the side of the road at reasonable intervals on motorways, accessible to their members. Members received a key to open the kiosk in which the phone was housed, and had to pay fourpence to make a call to the AA.

They looked at what they were trying to achieve and then surveyed what was already in existence, and could be utilised.

The solution they came up with was for Macmillan to join the AA and his driver to carry the key required to access the phone boxes. They would get a radio signal to the car if such an emergency was happening, and the driver would find the nearest AA telephone box.

The problem then arose that the driver may not have the four pennies required to make the call. After much deliberation, the MOD instructed drivers to make a reverse charge call.

We can see that the arrival of this solution is through the 3 Solutions Focus steps.

1. Describe what we want to achieve (the Prime Minister to be able to be in contact at short notice)
2. Identify what is working well (AA network of phones)
3. Take small steps (join the AA, equip the driver with the key, reverse charge calls if necessary)

New Way of Thinking

When we are focusing on the problem, we are often focusing on the "what-ifs". We think we are ahead of the game by doing this. "If I can cover all eventualities, I will know how to respond when they arise." This is unhelpful thinking and a complete waste of time. For starters, we can never know what may occur; we cannot possibly cover every eventuality; and we are wasting valuable time on overthinking situations that may never arise. We are concentrating on worst case scenarios, almost willing them to happen so that we can put our plans into action. However, those scenarios are unlikely to all happen, in which case the back-up actions are not going to be necessary (and yes, I do recognise that I have deliberately played the "what-if" game here myself). We have focused so much on those scenarios, that all we have left is the problem.

Stop focusing on what we don't know and focus only on what we do know.

We need to focus on our ultimate aim – what we want, what the ideal looks like.

Tool:

This tool is to allow you to start the process of Solutions Focus thinking.

Think of an issue which you want to develop. It may be an exercise that you do with the team, or may be one that you focus on yourself. In your staff team discuss the following questions and write up the consensus on a white board.

1. What are we seeking to achieve? What does the solution look like?
2. What personnel do we have available?
3. Now put a lot of detail in to describe exactly how your solution will look, and who will be involved. Put as much flesh to your vision as possible.

Remember, you are not trying to create an ultimate solution. You are working towards it by first recognising what you want to achieve and by then planning baby steps to move you closer to it.

That's just the start. Now you have to go about addressing the solution. Another whole team exercise can help you to address solutions.

Tool: The Scaling Question

In a room with a wide space mark out a line with masking tape, with equal marks from one to ten. With regard to a particular problem that you are in the process of solving, ask your team members to place themselves on the appropriate number where they think the team is. Ten being the best it can be and 1 the worst.

Now set the scene. A miracle has happened in our organisation (or project or team or whatever you are focussing on) after we went home last night, and everything was perfect when we got in to the office this morning. We weren't there so we don't know that the miracle happened. What will we see that tells us that the miracle has taken place?

Return to seats to the discuss.

Then delve, by asking questions about the miracle scenario, such as:

1. Were we in the same place last week (month/year) as we are after the miracle?
2. What has happened to change where we are now?
3. What was happening when we were higher up the scale?
4. What realistic step can we take to move up to the next rung of the scale?
5. How would we know if we had moved up the scale?
6. What needs to be in place for us to move up the scale?
7. What strengths and skills do we have in the team to help us move up the scale?

After a detailed discussion, return the team to the scale and identify where people are now.

When asking questions, construct them with all the usual When? What? How? Who? Which? You could also have questions that start with, "In what way…?" or, "Suppose that…?"

These are all questions which focus on solving a problem with a view to generating new thoughts.

The one question to never ask is the "Why?" question. It is accusatory, seeks blame and is provocative and adversarial. We can identify the Solutions Focus system as OSKAR.

Outcome – what is wanted

Scaling Questions – where are we in terms of outcome?

Know – gain an understanding of what put you at this point on the scale

Action – what are the next small achievable steps?

Review – what is better since last time? How was this achieved?

Results

It is common to find colleagues bickering about each other, or talking behind each other's backs. This is an indirect way to elevate themselves. By denigrating someone else, you are elevating yourself.

Turn it around. By training your staff to think differently you can get them to focus on all the positive points about each other – their attributes, their skillset, their experience and successes. In discussions about what colleagues are good at, we can start to see what they bring to the team and how they can be deployed effectively to utilise their skills appropriately. Forget the disparaging comments and the focus on failings; concentrate on the successes and positives.

When the whole staff team is thinking in this way, it promotes understanding, unity and consistency. Thinking starts to be aligned across the organisation with the result that there are fewer misunderstandings, greater cohesion and even greater camaraderie.

The staff will become more productive and the organisation will find that there is a lot of time saved. All that time focusing on the problem without moving forward is stultifying and demoralising.

Solutions Focus is all about moving forward and not trying to change the past. By all means use the past as a resource, but the past is your enemy; dialogue is your friend. There isn't one simple solution; it will emerge through dialogue – in plenum, listen to several ideas, allowing ideas to spark off other ideas and evolve. Solutions focus is a collaborative process.

Instead of debating whether we are glass-half-full or glass-half-empty people, start to turn our focus onto what is in the glass and what we are going to do with it.

14. Strategic Development

Running a company or charity without a strategy is like going in to battle and only fighting those who attack us.

In the above adage, if we have no strategy, we just face our known adversaries in battle, but then get attacked from behind. LinkedIn's webpage likens having no strategy to a pilot failing to fill the tank with fuel and then expecting autopilot to take over.

We sometimes are afraid of the term "strategic development". We know what we do; we are doing it reasonably well; we've been doing it for ages. Why do we need a strategy? We hear terms such as 5-year plan, mission statement and company vision and it frightens us.

Developing a strategy is important to begin to understand what we are doing, how we are doing it, and whether it is making the appropriate impact or having the desired effect. We also need something for new staff to refer to, existing staff to be motivated by, and replacement leadership to follow on from.

> **Story:**
>
> I spoke to someone recently who works for an ecological educational charity, Samantha.
>
> Her job is to recruit and train representatives from a variety of locations and backgrounds, who educate about ecological issues in schools nationally. She is very accomplished and comes from a professional background that has given her the experience and understanding to be able to lead on this project, and to initiate new methods and processes and introduce novel approaches.
>
> She has been in the job for two years, and is finding that she wants to challenge herself beyond what has now become mundane to her. On approaching the senior management for a copy of the Strategic Plan, she was told, "We don't need one right now. We know what we do. It's a long process, and needs to be signed off by the board."

In the above story, the organisation may know what they do, and its importance, and they have perfected their methodology over the years, but they have no idea why things work or don't work because they don't really have an idea of what they are aiming for. Equally, they have no idea if their stakeholders are satisfied with the organisation's approach and results because there are metrics or goals to measure against. Similarly, they don't know what direction they are heading for; just lurching from crisis to crisis or blindly doing what they have always done, without direction.

Every organisation should have a strategy to guide them to what they want to achieve so they can know when they are achieving it, know what the options are, understand the clientele and stakeholders, know the availability of staff and resources and so on. It also means that everyone in the organisation is working to unified plans and know that they are all striving for a common goal, and it gives direction and purpose to all staff.

It doesn't have to be rigid or constraining, but it should be something that guides towards what we are trying to achieve. It has to be flexible enough so that people joining the organisation are able to bring their personality and skillset to the benefit of the organisation.

In order to establish a strategic plan, you need to evaluate what is in place already. There are whole books on writing a strategic plan, creating a vision and a mission, interim plans and evaluation opportunities. However, I am going to try and make it really simple.

First do a SWOT analysis (Strengths, Weaknesses, Opportunities and Threats). Identify all of the aspects of each of these headings. It is usually preferable to do this as a team. A team will be able to generate a lot more ideas and discussion to populate these lists. Concentrate on each heading independently. Don't flit between them because it becomes confusing and loses focus.

Once you know what your strengths are, you can do more or similar things; you can capitalise on what is going well. Knowing your weaknesses helps to understand where improvements can be made. There is no point in throwing a lot of resources and staff into the weaknesses until you understand them and know how to address them, or perhaps just dispense with that side of things to concentrate on what is going well.

The opportunities are those things that you have yet to tap into. It might be a member of staff who has a particular skillset, or a new source of income. Whatever it is, when you recognise these opportunities, you know that there is scope for improving your provision or production.

The threats are those things which might prevent you from getting where you want to be. It might be a competitor in the business world, objections from the council or anything at all that might need to be overcome in order to proceed with your plans.

Strengths	Weaknesses
Opportunities	Threats

Aims and Objectives

Some people look at these and think that they are the same thing. They are decidedly not. Learn to differentiate and your Strategic Plan will practically write itself.

Aims

An aim is a target, a goal, a dream – something you are hoping that your organisation will achieve or become. There is just one aim that encompasses everything you intend for the organisation.

An example, using Samantha's story, might be: "Our aim is for Ecology Education Charity (EEC) to promote and educate about ecology across the country." Anyone reading this will see that it is a laudable aim but very woolly and there is no marker to tell us whether we have achieved that aim. It is just something in general that we are heading for.

Objectives

Objectives guide the process to achieve that aim. It always includes a verb – what you will do to achieve that aim, and a measure. There are usually a few objectives. It is important to have something to show for your endeavours. Objectives such as "I will scope..." or "We will search..." etc are meaningless. Appropriate objectives will include something to show for the work; they will be demonstrable. They will be SMART: Specific, Measurable, Achievable, Realistic, and Time bound. They are often interim or based on a specific project or end date.

For instance,

1. At the end of the project, we will have produced a list of at least thirty schools which are visited twice a year by our representatives.
2. By March 31st, we will have trained an additional 20 representatives.

3. By the end of their training course, all representatives on the course will demonstrate the ability to do a presentation at their school.
4. At the end of the year, our representatives will each produce a poster or essay illustrating their work this year.
5. By mid-July, every representative will have presented to at least two schools.
6. Within six months of completing their training, 15 of our new representatives will have presented in a school.

Note that these are all SMART. For the last one I could have written, "By the end of the training course, all representatives on the course will be able to…" This might be time bound, realistic and achievable. It might even be specific since we said "all". However, it is not measurable. How do we know that they can present? Only by watching them do it. Only by having them demonstrate it. Additionally, it's more realistic and achievable to give a number that is smaller than the whole.

Once you have mastered the SMART target, you are well on your way to achieving your Strategic Plan.

I am not focusing on the Vision (where you hope the organisation will be and what you hope it will achieve) and the Mission (a broad statement that describes what you set out to do, what your organisation represents). You need both of these, but I want to focus on developing a strategic plan, once you have both of these.

Exercise: Convert your organisational aim and mission to at least five SMART objectives.

If you do not have an organisational aim, write one now. Remember, this is a broad vision of what you do and what you are hoping to achieve. What you stand for and what people know you for.

If one doesn't exist, write a Mission as well.

Now write 5 SMART objectives using your Vision and Mission as your backdrop. Remember that objectives should include a time clause and a demonstrable verb, something you can see at the end, and measure. They are often sequential, so 1 has to be completed before 2 etc. However, this is not always the case.

Only you will know if they are realistic or achievable. The Specificity, Measurement and Time need to be written in to the objective.

1. _____

2. _____

3. _____

4. _____

5. _____

Writing clear objectives is important because it is these that will inform the work that you do. You can now adapt this exercise to be used on the leadership or staff team.

The steps to writing a strategic plan

1. Identify where you are now
2. Discuss and agree where you would like to be
3. Agree upon a Vision and a Mission Statement
4. SWOT analysis
5. Identify direction options
6. Write a list of SMART objectives and use them to write the strategy
7. Communicate the strategy to board and staff
8. Implement the strategy

15. Staff

"I have always been of the opinion that consistency is the last refuge of the unimaginative."

Oscar Wilde

Inducting new staff members does not mean hand-holding. All too often people join the team or organisation and feel that they can just coast, because their introduction to the team, project or organisation has involved being told what to do and how to do it. Hand-holding is not helpful – either for the team or organisation or for the employee themselves.

Being too prescriptive can often delay their development in the role. They are slower to take ownership of the work, relying instead on the help that you are offering.

Induction

The training of new staff should be experiential, immersive and offer opportunities to try and to fail. The failures themselves are instructional.

"A learning experience is one of those things that says, 'You know that thing you just did? Don't do that.'"

Douglas Adams

Story:

Jason started a new job, taking over from George as Executive Director of a small national charity. He was an experienced director and had ideas of how he would like to take the organisation forward.

The first week of his employment was to be a "handover" week. George would explain the systems and go through the workings of the organisation, and generally introduce him to what needs to be done. Jason was looking forward to this week, expecting it to give him the skills to start the job with immediate impact.

He arrived diligently for his first day and found that the "handover" was a 62-page booklet explaining every minutia of every detail of every action that he will ever need to take – all the payment procedures, accounting, every nuanced personality trait of every member of staff and board member, how e-mails are stored and how follow-up is conducted and countless other administrative details.

Yes, they are important details and Jason does have to take them on board. However, the handover week consisted entirely of sitting and listening to George go through the booklet and painstakingly explain everything that was in it. There were no demonstrations and no opportunities to try out the systems.

Unsurprisingly, by the end of the week, Jason was absolutely exhausted and remembered very little.

> Admittedly, George gave him opportunity to ask questions, but Jason had really not taken enough in to have any questions.

The saying goes:

"Tell Me and I Forget;
Teach Me and I May Remember;
Involve Me and I Learn."

Jason certainly hadn't learned anything, and remembered very little. There was no involvement, no teaching, just a mind-numbing collection of facts.

George would have been much more effective if he had shown Jason where to find the booklet, identified some key information for Jason to assimilate, drawn up a few simple flow charts and let him access the document as and when it was needed. The induction week would have been much more effective had Jason had the opportunity to experience doing some of the tasks.

In fact, from my experience as a teacher, I know that we retain information as follows:

Activity	%
Lecture	5
Reading	10
Audio Visual	20
Demonstration	30
Discussion Group	50
Practice Doing	75
Teach Others	90

Responsibility

In the above story, George had been doing the job for years and thought that the way he does things is the way things are done. He thought that if he just disgorges everything in his head and implants it all into Jason's head, the organisation will go on just fine and everything would continue working as it had, *ad infinitum*.

What he failed to take account of was that every employee and every leader brings a bit of themselves to the job. They rely, not only on their training and skillset but also on their experience, creativity, ideas and temperament. George had been the first ED of this organisation and had made it his own. What he failed to recognise was that Jason had new ideas and was keen to implement new ways of doing things.

By all means give the new employee the rundown on the organisation, but then let them fly. Allow them to develop their own systems. Give them responsibility, not only of their role in the organisation but also their own development. Along with personal development comes organisational development.

Knowledge Acquisition

The new recruit will need to acquire the knowledge of the organisation. They need to know how things get done, who to turn to for what, and how to access information. They also need to develop in the job and make it their own. Mostly, they need to acquire the knowledge they need by doing the job and imprinting the experiences in their brains. It takes time.

Achievements

It is obviously important to recognise achievements and make sure that every member of staff is working effectively and equitably. However, there can sometimes be too much emphasis on measuring or checking on achievements with little attention to the way the work is being done, its value to the stakeholders or the impact that that work is having on the organisation as a whole. Most importantly, we need to value our people.

Story:

Greg was a staff member in a large organisation. He headed up a particularly niche area of the work, but had no-one else in his department. He had some good ideas which he implemented, and he ran some successful projects. However, because he worked alone, he often had to either consult other teams for advice on how to proceed, or collaborate with them on projects.

The leadership ran a tight ship. They conducted quarterly assessments of the work that everyone was doing, to construct a report to the board. Team leaders added to a shared document which was then constructed into a report by the CEO. Greg was often left floundering with a short list of his achievements. He was keen to make it look like he was working hard (which he was), and he found himself taking credit for colleagues' work – often.

What this demonstrates is that when leadership doesn't acknowledge and value their staff, but only their output, there is a temptation to exaggerate one's performance

---

Greg didn't need an "employee of the year award", nor a cheap promotional pen. What he needed was for the leadership to recognise the great work he was doing, in particularly trying circumstances; the very positive alliances he was forming in pursuit of a great project, and the collaborative work that he was executing. A simple list of achievements doesn't highlight these things; it's people who do. What Greg needed was to feel recognised and valued, and to be part of a team.

It's not always necessary for a formal commendation or a mention in the staff briefing. What we all need is just a simple acknowledgement from our colleagues and leaders, for something that we have done or even for continuing to do our job consistently.

If we are going to recognise achievements, it's not good enough to commend for having completed the project – like the finance director at the beginning of the book who got his cheap promotional pen for having done the accounts. If we are commending publicly (which I really am not advising) make sure that everyone is being individually commended and that no-one is left out. And make that commendation quantifiable and identifiable – a specific project with a measurable outcome.

It is also important to recognise that some pieces of work are self-contained short projects while others might take years. For instance, the fundraising goals of a charity might take years to achieve. In these cases, we can recognise the interim achievements.

Over the years, I have worked in a variety of organisations and have come across some lovely, simple ways of recognising staff.

I once visited an organisation whose very charismatic new leader recognised that changes needed to be made and was doing his best to understand the organisation that he was leading. He placed a suggestion box in the foyer, publicising it to all of his staff and asking them to use it freely to make whatever suggestions that they wished to see implemented. This was hugely encouraging for his team who were hopeful of meaningful change. The only problem was that he literally never looked at the suggestions in the box. This was disheartening for his staff, who were hoping for some positive changes to happen. Not only were the changes not forthcoming, but the efforts of the staff members to make suggestions were not even acknowledged.

I believe that a new leader in an organisation should find ways to assess the strengths of each of their members of staff. This can be done through regular performance reviews, but there are many other ways that can be employed to get the most information about each of the staff members.

- Ask them; start with a transparent conversation
- Watch how they perform in meetings and with colleagues
- Construct a SWOT analysis for each person, which you can complete together, and build over time
- Put them in real or simulated situations to gauge reaction
- Ask for clients or stakeholders' feedback

Schools, for instance, always have a way of commending colleagues for their work. In one school I visited, there was an entire wall of written notes to teachers from the pupils. The school had pre-printed cards to fill in with name and reason for the commendation. Every day, every pupil and every staff member would walk past and see the value that the pupils place in their teachers, and their appreciation of the good work that the teachers have done for them. A reminder to the teachers that the work they are doing is paying dividends.

Another idea in some schools is the staff shout-outs. A few minutes is taken in weekly briefings for staff to pat each other on the back publicly for something that an individual has done that week, or an achievement made with a particular pupil. The staff member being praised gets not only the feelgood factor from having done well, and the recognition by the colleague who witnessed it, but the entire staff has been told. This is hugely motivating. Recognition doesn't need to come from the management.

When I was running a youth movement many years ago, I witnessed a lovely event. At the end of a residential seminar, the group held a candle evening. This was a programmed event for the last night of the seminar. The whole group sat around in a circle. Lights were dimmed and a lit candle was held by the leader. He proceeded to talk about every individual and to point out something positive for each of them. He then passed the candle to the next person who did the same, until every person in the circle had had a turn to speak. The only two rules were that only the person with the candle was allowed to speak and that speakers were not allowed to make negative comments. At the end of the evening, every person had the opportunity to hear many good things about themselves – a truly bolstering experience.

A reminder that we all shine when we are acknowledged and commended.

In short, we all thrive on recognition. We work better when we are collaborating, and competition is demotivating.